The Old Farmer's Almanac

{ FAVORITE }

COOKIES

From the Publishers of

THE OLD FARMER'S ALMANAC

Dublin, New Hampshire 03444

www.almanac.com

Contents

54
CUTOUT COOKIES

Editor: Debra Keller
Art Director: Margo Letourneau
Editorial Staff: Susan Peery, Mare-Anne Jarvela,
Randy Miller
Copy Editor: Ellen Bingham
Production: Susan Gross, David Ziarnowski,
Lucille Rines, Rachel Kipka, Nathaniel Stout
Group Publisher: John Pierce
Publisher: Sherin Wight

Editorial and Publishing Offices:
P.O. Box 520, Main Street, Dublin, NH 03444
Phone: 603-563-8111; fax: 603-563-8252
Web site: www.almanac.com

Copyright © 2000 by Yankee Publishing Incorporated
PRINTED IN U.S.A.

To order *The Old Farmer's Almanac Favorite Cookies* and other
Almanac products, call 800-223-3166 or visit our Web site at
www.almanac.com.

Cover photo and inside photography by Laurie Vogt

Bar Cookies

🖤 Bar cookies are generally made from a batter that is spread in a pan, then baked, cooled, and often stored right in the pan. In this way, they are the simplest of cookies, requiring little handling—and can be a quick route to satisfying a sweet-treat craving.

PHOTO

Rocky-Road Brownies. Recipe on page 8.

PEANUT-BUTTER BROWNIES

When you combine chocolate and peanut butter, you can't miss. These brownies are destined to be popular.

1/3 cup all-purpose flour

1/4 teaspoon baking powder

1/4 teaspoon baking soda

1/4 cup (1/2 stick) unsalted butter

3 ounces unsweetened chocolate, chopped

3/4 cup packed light-brown sugar

2 large eggs

2 teaspoons vanilla extract

1/3 cup creamy peanut butter

1/3 cup peanut-butter chips

Adjust rack to lower third of oven and preheat oven to 350°F. Line an 8x8-inch baking pan with aluminum foil. Press foil into corners and up the sides of the pan.

Whisk together the flour, baking powder, and baking soda in a small bowl. In a small, heavy-bottomed saucepan, melt the butter and the chocolate. Pour into a mixing bowl and stir in the brown sugar. Add the eggs, thoroughly blending into the mixture. Stir in the vanilla and peanut butter, then the flour mixture.

Spread batter evenly into prepared pan. Bake for 22 minutes. Cool in the pan on a rack. When cool, mark off 1-1/2-inch squares with the tip of a sharp paring knife. Using the handle of a wooden spoon, poke a hole into the center of each brownie; fill hole with peanut-butter chips, flat side up to fit flush with the surface of the brownies. Cut through the markings to form squares.

Makes 20.

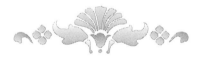

GINGER DATE BARS

These chewy bars, spiked with ginger and the crunch of nuts, are a welcome addition to any sweet table.

3/4 cup all-purpose flour

1/4 teaspoon baking powder

1/4 cup (1/2 stick) unsalted butter

1 cup sugar

2 large eggs

1 cup chopped walnuts

1 cup chopped dates

3 tablespoons chopped crystallized ginger

Adjust rack to lower third of oven and preheat oven to 350°F. Grease and flour the bottom of a 9x9-inch baking pan; line pan with baking parchment or waxed paper.

Whisk the flour and the baking powder in a small bowl to combine. In a larger bowl, beat the butter and sugar until creamy. Add the eggs and beat just until blended. Stir in the flour mixture, then the nuts, dates, and ginger.

Bake for 30 minutes, or until light golden on top. Let cool in pan for 5 minutes, then invert immediately onto a sheet of baking parchment or waxed paper. Lift off the paper used during baking. While warm, cut into uniform bars with a sharp knife.

Makes 35 squares (1-1/2 inches).

PISTACHIO DRIED-CRANBERRY BARS

Beautifully seasonal, these bars are a delicious treat for the holidays.

DOUGH:

2 cups all-purpose flour

1/8 teaspoon baking powder

1/4 teaspoon salt

3/4 cup sugar

3/4 cup (1-1/2 sticks) unsalted butter

1 large egg, beaten slightly

2 teaspoons finely grated orange zest

TOPPING:

1/4 cup (1/2 stick) unsalted butter, softened

2 cups unsifted confectioners' sugar

1/8 teaspoon salt

3 tablespoons fresh orange juice

3 ounces shelled pistachios, chopped

3 ounces dried cranberries, chopped

Adjust rack to lower third of oven and preheat oven to 350°F. Grease and flour a 15x10x1-inch jelly-roll pan.

For dough: Place flour, baking powder, salt, and sugar into a food processor, and process just to blend ingredients. Add butter in pieces and process until mixture resembles corn-meal. In a small bowl, whisk together egg and zest. With processor running, pour egg mixture down feed tube and process just until ingredients form a ball. Press dough into baking pan. Bake for 15 to 17 minutes, or until top is ivory-colored and edges and bottoms are pale golden. Remove from oven and place onto a wire rack to cool.

For topping: Combine first four ingredients and beat until smooth and creamy. Spread frosting over cooled cookie. Sprinkle on pistachios and cranberries, gently pressing them into frosting. Cut into bars or triangles.

Makes about 4 dozen.

A NEAT TIP

❤ Grating citrus zest is much neater and easier if you first cover the grater surface with a piece of plastic wrap. When finished, peel off the plastic and gather up the zest with a rubber scraper. Change plastic between fruits.

ROCKY-ROAD BROWNIES

Favorite flavors take a new form in this easy-to-whip-up comfort-food treat. (See photo, page 4.)

3/4 cup all-purpose flour

1/4 teaspoon baking soda

1/8 teaspoon salt

6 tablespoons unsalted butter

3 ounces unsweetened chocolate, coarsely chopped

1 cup sugar

2 large eggs, lightly beaten

1 teaspoon vanilla extract

1 cup miniature marshmallows

1/2 cup semisweet chocolate chips

1/2 cup finely chopped pecans

Adjust rack to lower third of oven and preheat oven to 325°F. Grease and flour an 8x8-inch baking pan.

Sift flour, baking soda, and salt onto a sheet of waxed paper, and set aside. In a medium saucepan over low heat, melt butter and chocolate and stir until smooth. Pour into a large bowl, stir in sugar, and let stand for 5 minutes. Stir in eggs, then vanilla and flour mixture. Spread batter evenly in pan and bake for 25 minutes (do not overbake).

In a bowl, toss together marshmallows and chocolate chips, then scatter mixture over hot brownie in pan. Scatter chopped nuts over marshmallows and chocolate chips, and return pan to oven for only 5 minutes. Cool thoroughly on a wire rack before cutting into squares.

Makes 1-1/2 to 2 dozen.

S'MORE SQUARES

The traditional campfire treat grows up without losing any of its youthful appeal. No wonder everyone wants s'more S'Mores!

6 tablespoons unsalted butter

3 ounces unsweetened chocolate

1 cup sugar

2 large eggs

1 teaspoon vanilla extract

1/2 cup all-purpose flour

1/4 teaspoon salt

TOPPING:

1 cup miniature marshmallows

1 cup milk-chocolate chips

4 large graham crackers, broken into small pieces

Adjust rack to lower third of oven and preheat oven to 375°F. In a small saucepan over low heat, melt the butter and chocolate together. Remove from heat and stir in the sugar. Pour into a 3-quart mixing bowl and set aside to cool for about 5 minutes. Add the eggs and vanilla to the cooled chocolate mixture, stirring just until blended. Stir in the flour and salt. Spread batter in a greased 8x8-inch pan. Bake for 15 minutes.

For topping: Sprinkle individual ingredients over brownie, and bake for 5 minutes longer. Cool in pan on a wire rack before cutting into squares.

Makes 16 squares.

TROPICAL CONGO BARS

A popular cookie goes tropical with macadamia nuts and coconut.

3/4 cup (1-1/2 sticks) unsalted butter, melted
  and cooled

2-3/4 cups (1 pound) packed light-brown sugar,
  free of lumps

3 large eggs

2-3/4 cups all-purpose flour

2-1/2 teaspoons baking powder

1/2 teaspoon salt

1 cup chocolate chips

1 cup coarsely chopped macadamia nuts

1/3 cup apricot or pineapple jam

1-1/2 cups toasted, shredded coconut

Grease a 15x10x1-inch pan. Adjust rack to lower third of oven and preheat oven to 325°F.

In a large bowl, mix together the melted butter, brown sugar, and eggs just until blended. Sift the flour, baking powder, and salt (omit salt if using salted nuts) into another bowl, and add this to the egg mixture. Stir in the chocolate chips and nuts. Spread dough in the pan (it's sticky, so you may want to pat it out with your fingertips). Bake for 30 minutes, or until golden on the surface. It will still look soft. Remove pan from oven and place on a wire rack. Brush uncut bars with jam, and sprinkle with toasted coconut. Cut while still warm.

Makes 50 small bars.

TOASTING TIP

❤ Toast coconut in a dry, nonstick pan over low heat, stirring often, until lightly colored.

COCONUT PECAN SQUARES

Baker Jean Camden advises to be sure and use the dark- and light-brown sugars as directed to get the best results with these delectable little bars.

1/2 cup (1 stick) butter

1/2 cup packed dark-brown sugar

1 cup all-purpose flour

2 eggs

1 cup packed light-brown sugar

1 cup chopped pecans

1/2 cup shredded coconut tossed with 2 tablespoons
  flour

1 teaspoon vanilla extract

pinch of salt

confectioners' sugar

Cream butter and dark-brown sugar, then add the 1 cup flour and mix well. Press into a greased 8x8-inch pan and bake at 350°F for 20 minutes. Meanwhile, beat the eggs until frothy. Gradually add light-brown sugar and beat until thick. Add pecans, coconut tossed with flour, vanilla, and salt. Mix well. Spread over crust and bake for 20 minutes longer, or until brown. Cool on rack. Sprinkle with confectioners' sugar and cut into 1-inch squares.

Makes about 36 squares.

Cherry Streusel Bars

Plan to pack these fruity bars into your next picnic basket.

1 cup all-purpose flour

1-1/2 cups chopped walnuts

2/3 cup sugar

1/2 teaspoon cinnamon

1/4 teaspoon salt

1/8 teaspoon baking powder

1/2 cup (1 stick) plus 2 tablespoons unsalted butter, chilled and cut into 1/4-inch slices

1 large egg yolk

1 cup cherry preserves

STREUSEL:

1/2 cup unsifted all-purpose flour

1/2 cup chopped walnuts

1/2 cup plus 2 tablespoons uncooked rolled oats

1/2 cup packed brown sugar

1/2 teaspoon baking powder

1/2 teaspoon cinnamon

1/8 teaspoon salt

5 tablespoons butter, softened

Preheat oven to 350°F. Blend flour, nuts, sugar, cinnamon, salt, and baking powder in a food processor until nuts are finely ground. Add butter, and process until the consistency of coarse meal. Add egg yolk, and process just until mixture forms a ball. With floured fingertips, pat dough into an ungreased 9x9-inch pan. Spread preserves over dough.

For streusel: Combine all streusel topping ingredients except butter, and beat with an electric mixer at low speed. Add butter, and mix until consistency of crumbly granola. Sprinkle over preserves to cover, but don't pat it down. Bake for 45 minutes, or until light golden. Cool completely before cutting.

Makes 16 bars.

EASIER CUTTING

When cutting sticky bar cookies, wipe the knife with a damp paper towel after each cut.

CHOCOLATE MUD-SEASON BARS

*Here's some mud you won't mind sinking (your teeth) into—a gooey, mudlike layer of chocolate around
lots of walnuts on top of a graham cracker crust. The ultimate!*

CRUST:

8 whole graham crackers

1/4 cup packed light-brown sugar

1/4 teaspoon cinnamon

1/4 cup (1/2 stick) unsalted butter, melted

FILLING:

1/2 cup (1 stick) unsalted butter

6 ounces semisweet chocolate, coarsely chopped

3/4 cup sugar

1/3 cup unsweetened cocoa powder

2 large eggs, at room temperature

1/4 cup all-purpose flour

1 cup coarsely chopped walnuts

For crust: Combine crackers, brown sugar, and cinnamon in the bowl of a food processor and make fine crumbs. Transfer to a bowl, stir in melted butter, and mix well with hands until evenly blended. Pat into bottom and partially up sides of a greased 8x8-inch pan. Bake crust at 350°F for 10 minutes. Cool. Lower heat to 325°.

For filling: Melt butter in medium saucepan. Turn off heat and add chocolate. Wait 5 minutes for chocolate to melt, then whisk to smooth. Scrape chocolate into medium bowl. Combine sugar and cocoa in a small bowl and whisk into melted chocolate. Gently beat the eggs to liquefy, then whisk into batter just until smooth. Stir in flour, then nuts.

Scrape filling onto crust and smooth with a spoon. Bake for 40 minutes. Cool to room temperature, then refrigerate for 1 to 2 hours before slicing. They're at their best if they aren't too cold.

Makes 16 small bars.

MINT CHOCOLATE-CHIP BROWNIES

What to do with summer's most prolific herb? Look no further. Bring on the vanilla ice cream!

2/3 cup sugar

1/4 cup packed fresh mint leaves, or 1-1/2 tablespoons
    dried mint

1/2 cup (1 stick) unsalted butter

4 ounces semisweet chocolate, coarsely chopped

2 large eggs, lightly beaten

1 teaspoon vanilla extract

2/3 cup all-purpose flour

1/4 teaspoon salt

1 cup mint chocolate chips

Grease and flour an 8x8-inch pan and preheat oven to 325°F. Combine the sugar and mint in the bowl of a food processor and process for 30 to 60 seconds until the mint is pulverized. Set aside. Melt the butter in a 2-quart saucepan over low heat. Turn off the heat and add the chocolate. Set aside for 5 minutes to melt. Whisk chocolate to smooth, then stir in the mint sugar mixture. Whisk in the eggs and vanilla.

Mix together the flour and salt, then stir into the chocolate mixture until evenly blended. Fold in the mint chocolate chips. Scrape the batter into the prepared pan and bake for 35 minutes. When done, the surface will be quite soft. Cool overnight on a rack before slicing.

Makes 16 small brownies.

DUTCH APPLE-CRUMB BARS

Fresh fall apples between a buttery crust and cinnamon crumb topping. Yum!

CRUST:

1-1/2 cups all-purpose flour

1/3 cup sugar

1/4 teaspoon salt

1/2 cup (1 stick) cold unsalted butter

1 egg yolk

2-1/2 tablespoons cold water

FILLING:

3 cups peeled, cored, chopped apples

1/2 cup chopped pitted dates

1/4 cup sugar

2 teaspoons lemon juice

TOPPING:

1/2 cup all-purpose flour

1/3 cup uncooked rolled oats

1/3 cup packed light-brown sugar

1/2 teaspoon cinnamon

pinch of salt

1/4 cup (1/2 stick) cold unsalted butter, cut into
   4 pieces

Preheat oven to 350°F and grease a 9x9-inch pan. For crust: Combine flour, sugar, and salt in a food processor. Pulse to blend, then add butter in pieces. Process for about 10 seconds to make a fine meal. Blend yolk and water. Pour over dry ingredients and process until damp crumbs form. Pat crumbs into bottom and halfway up sides of pan. Bake for 25 minutes.

■ For filling: Mix apples, dates, sugar, and lemon juice. Spread evenly over crust.

■ For topping: Combine flour, oats, brown sugar, cinnamon, and salt. Add butter and rub it in to make moist crumbs. Cover apples with topping and pat gently. Bake for 40 minutes, or until golden brown. Cool completely before slicing.

Makes 16 bars.

CUTTING COMMENTS

♥ You can cut bar cookies cleanly and easily with a thin-bladed dough scraper. Try it!

CHOCOLATE MINT STICKS

These rich confections look beautiful on a tea tray or plate of Christmas cookies.

2 eggs, beaten

1/2 cup (1 stick) butter, melted

2 squares unsweetened chocolate, melted

1 cup sugar

1/2 teaspoon vanilla extract

1/2 cup all-purpose flour

FROSTING:

2 tablespoons butter

1 cup sifted confectioners' sugar

1 tablespoon light cream

1/2 teaspoon peppermint flavoring, or 1 to 2
    tablespoons crème de menthe

1/2 square unsweetened chocolate, melted

1-1/2 tablespoons butter, melted

Combine all ingredients except flour; beat well. Blend in flour. Pour into a greased and floured 9x9-inch pan. Bake at 350°F for 25 minutes. Cool.

For frosting: Mix butter, confectioners' sugar, cream, and peppermint flavoring. Spread over cooled baked layer. When frosting is firm, mix melted chocolate and butter, and drizzle over all. Place into refrigerator until firm. Cut into small sticks or squares and put into small cupcake papers.

Makes about 4-1/2 dozen.

OATMEAL CHOCOLATE BARS

A dense cookie base of oats and brown sugar is topped by a fudgy chocolate filling—better than a candy bar!

FILLING:

2 tablespoons butter or margarine

6 ounces chocolate chips

1 can (5-1/3 ounces) evaporated milk

1/4 cup sugar

1/2 cup chopped nuts

BASE:

1/2 cup (1 stick) butter or margarine

1 cup packed brown sugar

1 egg

1 teaspoon vanilla extract

1-1/4 cups all-purpose flour

1/2 teaspoon baking soda

2 cups uncooked quick-cooking rolled oats

For filling: In a heavy saucepan, combine butter, chocolate chips, evaporated milk, and sugar. Bring to a rolling boil, stirring constantly. Remove from heat. Stir in nuts and cool.

For base: Cream butter and brown sugar. Add egg and vanilla, and beat until light and fluffy. Stir in flour, baking soda, and 1-3/4 cups of the oats until well blended. Press 2/3 of this mixture into the bottom of a greased 9x9-inch pan. Spread with cooled chocolate filling. Mix remaining 1/4 cup oats with remainder of cookie base, and crumble over filling. Bake at 350°F for 25 to 30 minutes.

Makes 36 bars.

TOFFEE SQUARES

These easy-to-make squares have a buttery base topped with a thin layer of chocolate and nuts.

1 cup (2 sticks) butter

1 cup packed light-brown sugar

1 egg yolk

2 cups all-purpose flour

1 teaspoon vanilla extract

6 ounces semisweet chocolate chips

2/3 cup finely chopped nuts

Cream butter and brown sugar. Add egg yolk. Add flour and vanilla, and stir until well blended. Spread dough into a greased 15x10x1-inch jelly-roll pan and bake at 350°F for 15 to 20 minutes, or until golden brown. Remove from oven and immediately sprinkle chocolate chips on top of crust. Allow chocolate to soften, and spread evenly. Sprinkle with chopped nuts and press nuts lightly into chocolate, using the bottom of a glass. Cool, then cut into squares.

Makes at least 3 dozen, depending on size.

APRICOT OATMEAL BARS

You can vary the type of preserves used in the bars; raspberry makes a delicious bar as well.

DOUGH:

1-1/4 cups all-purpose flour

1-1/4 cups uncooked rolled oats

1/2 cup sugar

3/4 cup (1-1/2 sticks) butter, melted

1/2 teaspoon baking soda

1/4 teaspoon salt

2 teaspoons vanilla extract

FILLING:

10 ounces apricot preserves

1/2 cup shredded coconut

For dough: In a large mixing bowl, combine all dough ingredients and mix until crumbly. Reserve 1 cup of the mixture, and press the remainder into a greased 13x9-inch pan.

For filling: Spread the apricot preserves to within 1/2 inch of the edge of the crumb base; sprinkle with the reserved crumbs and the coconut. Bake at 350°F for about 25 minutes, or until edges are lightly browned.

Makes at least 3 dozen.

SWEDISH WHITE BROWNIES

Chewy and fragrant with almonds, these bars stir together in minutes and taste great with tea or coffee.

2 eggs

1 cup sugar

1/3 cup oil

1 teaspoon almond extract

1 cup all-purpose flour

sliced almonds and extra sugar, for garnish

Mix together all ingredients except the last, and pour into an 8x8-inch pan. Sprinkle with sliced almonds and sugar. Bake at 350°F for 25 to 30 minutes. Allow to cool in pan before cutting into bars.

Makes 16 brownies.

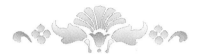

BEST BROWNIES

Everybody has a favorite brownie recipe, but these are hard to beat!

1 cup (2 sticks) butter, softened

2 cups sugar

1 tablespoon corn syrup

2/3 cup cocoa

4 eggs

1 teaspoon vanilla extract

1-1/2 cups all-purpose flour

1 teaspoon baking powder

Combine first 6 ingredients. In a separate bowl, combine flour and baking powder, and add to batter, mixing well. Pour into a 13x9-inch greased pan. Bake at 350°F for about 30 minutes. Allow to cool in pan before cutting into bars.

Makes 24 brownies.

HINT

❤ When baking brownies, use sifted cocoa powder instead of flour to dust the baking pan.

APRICOT ALMOND BARS

Carolyn Rosen won second prize with these delicious nut bars in the 1989 Old Farmer's Almanac Holiday
Cookies and Bars Recipe Contest.

TOPPING:

1-1/2 cups sugar

3 cups sliced blanched almonds

4 egg whites (save 2 yolks for crust)

2 tablespoons all-purpose flour

1/2 teaspoon cinnamon

1/4 teaspoon freshly grated nutmeg

CRUST:

2-1/2 cups all-purpose flour

1/2 cup sugar

1 cup (2 sticks) butter

2 egg yolks

APRICOT GLAZE:

1/2 cup apricot preserves

1 tablespoon water

CHOCOLATE GLAZE:

3 ounces semisweet chocolate

1 ounce unsweetened chocolate

For topping: In top of a double boiler over hot water, combine all ingredients. Cook, stirring occasionally, until mixture reaches 110°F on a candy thermometer. Remove from heat and set aside.

For crust: In a large bowl, combine flour and sugar. Cut in butter until mixture is crumbly. Add egg yolks. With hands, mix into a smooth dough. Line a jelly-roll pan (15x10x1-inch) with foil, and press dough into prepared pan. Prick dough with a fork and bake at 350°F for 15 minutes. Remove from oven and spread almond topping over crust. Return to oven and bake for 20 minutes longer.

For apricot glaze: Meanwhile, in a small saucepan, melt the apricot preserves with water over low heat. Strain through a fine sieve. Brush glaze over baked almond topping immediately after pan comes out of oven. Cool pan on rack. Cut into 2-inch squares when cool.

For chocolate glaze: In top of a double boiler over hot water, melt semisweet and unsweetened chocolate together. Drizzle on top of cookies. Allow to set.

Makes about 6 dozen.

MAPLE-PECAN STICKY BARS

At sugaring time or any old time, nothing beats the great taste of these gooey-good maple bars in a buttery shortbread crust.

CRUST:

1-1/4 cups all-purpose flour

1/3 cup sugar

1/8 teaspoon salt

6 tablespoons cold unsalted butter, cut up

1 egg yolk mixed with 1 tablespoon cold water

FILLING:

1/3 cup pure maple syrup

1/4 cup packed light-brown sugar

2 tablespoons unsalted butter

2 tablespoons heavy cream

1 cup chopped toasted pecans

Preheat oven to 350°F and grease an 8x8-inch pan.

For crust: Put flour, sugar, and salt into a food processor and mix briefly. Add butter and process for about 10 seconds, or until mixture resembles coarse meal. With machine running, add yolk and water to dry ingredients. Process briefly, just until dough starts to clump together. (Dough may also be mixed by hand or with an electric mixer.) Empty dough into pan and press into bottom and halfway up sides. Bake for 25 minutes, then cool on a rack.

For filling: Combine maple syrup, brown sugar, butter, and cream in a small saucepan. Bring to a boil, and boil for 2 minutes. Stir in nuts. Scrape filling into crust, and bake for 15 minutes. Cool on a rack.

Makes 16 small bars.

BEACH BLONDIES

These are a snap to bake, cut, and wrap the day before your next beach trip. Refrigerate overnight and they'll travel well.

1/2 cup (1 stick) unsalted butter, softened

1 cup packed light-brown sugar

1/2 cup smooth natural peanut butter

2 large eggs

1-1/2 teaspoons vanilla extract

1 cup all-purpose flour

1/2 teaspoon baking powder

1/4 teaspoon salt

1/2 teaspoon cinnamon

1/2 cup chopped roasted peanuts

1/2 cup chocolate chips

Preheat oven to 350°F and grease an 8x8- or 9x9-inch pan. Cream the butter, brown sugar, and peanut butter until smooth. Beat in the eggs and vanilla. In a separate bowl, sift flour, baking powder, salt, and cinnamon. Add dry ingredients to the creamed mixture along with peanuts and chocolate chips. Stir until smooth. Scrape batter into pan and smooth with a fork. Bake for 30 to 35 minutes; the smaller pan will take longer. Cool thoroughly in the pan on a rack before slicing.

Makes 9 large or 12 medium bars.

PUMPKIN CHEESECAKE BARS

You've had the pie, now try the cheesecake in these luscious bars that are the shade of a New England autumn hillside.

CRUST:

1 package (1/3 pound) graham crackers

1/3 cup packed light-brown sugar

1/2 teaspoon cinnamon

5 tablespoons unsalted butter, melted

FILLING:

8 ounces cream cheese, softened

2/3 cup packed light-brown sugar

1 large egg

1 egg yolk

1 teaspoon vanilla extract

1 tablespoon all-purpose flour

1/2 teaspoon EACH cinnamon, ginger, and nutmeg

3/4 cup canned pumpkin

1/3 cup heavy cream

Preheat oven to 350°F and grease a 9x9-inch pan.

For crust: Break the crackers into a food processor. Add brown sugar and cinnamon, and process to a fine meal. Add melted butter and process again. Press crust into the bottom and slightly up sides of pan. Bake for 10 minutes and cool. Reduce oven temperature to 325°F.

For filling: Cream the cream cheese, brown sugar, egg, and egg yolk. Blend in the vanilla. Blend in remaining ingredients until smooth. Pour into crust and bake for 45 minutes. Cool on a rack. Refrigerate for at least 4 hours before slicing.

Makes 9 bars.

Ten Things Cookie Bakers Really Ought to Know

1 Organize! Clutter is your worst enemy. You can't bake if the counter is a mess, the bottle of vanilla extract is hiding, and there's no place to put the cooling rack. Clear your work area before you begin, and get out all the ingredients. Put each one away as you use it, so you don't forget what you've used. Rinse bowls and utensils as you go.

2 Read the recipe through before you do anything. As you read, check your supply of staples (flour, sugar, butter) and watch for any unusual ingredients, steps, or equipment that might trip you up. For example, if the dough has to chill for 12 hours, you should know this before you start, in case you need the cookies by noon today.

3 Insist on good fresh ingredients. Spices lose their flavor over time; if you've had them around since last December, replace them. Use fresh local eggs if you can find them. Unsalted ("sweet") butter is preferable to salted; it tastes cleaner, sweeter, and fresher than salted butter—and often it is. Because salt acts as a preservative, salted butter can be warehoused longer than unsalted.

4 If you forget to soften your butter ahead of time, cut the stick(s) into thin pats and place them on a room-temperature plate. Leave in a warmish spot for 10 minutes or so, until the butter yields to gentle finger pressure. If a recipe calls for softened butter, it doesn't have to be squishy soft.

5 When a recipe calls for toasted nuts (incidentally, that's 8 to 10 minutes in a 350°F oven), make sure they're thoroughly cooled before adding them to dough. Adding hot nuts to a dough could melt the butter and drastically change the texture of your cookies, probably not for the better.

6 If you don't already own them, buy yourself a couple of good baking sheets. Thin, flimsy sheets don't diffuse heat well or evenly and can result in scorched cookie bottoms. Tinned steel and anodized aluminum are two good material choices. Neither is inexpensive, but they'll last. Look for them in gourmet kitchen shops. While you're there, invest in a heavy-duty stainless steel cooling rack that's large enough to hold 2 to 3 dozen cookies.

7 Generally speaking, bake only one sheet of cookies at a time, on the center rack. This allows for the most-even baking.

8 If you own only one cookie sheet, cool it to room temperature between batches. This prevents the butter from melting out of the dough and puddling up on the sheet.

9 As a rule, let cookies cool on the baking sheet for 1 or 2 minutes, just long enough to firm them slightly and make it easier to slide them off the sheet and onto a rack.

10 Most cookies ship well. For best results, however, choose a relatively firm or dense type of cookie. Wrap cookies individually in waxed paper and pack them snugly in a tin. Pack the tin inside a bigger box, cushioned on all sides with additional waxed paper. And it never hurts to be nice to the postal clerk.

–Ken Haedrich

Hand-Shaped Cookies

❤ Sometimes called molded cookies, these are made from a stiff dough that is formed by hand into little balls, crescents, canes, and other shapes, or forced through a cookie press. Handle the dough as little as possible and keep it chilled.

PHOTO

Poppy-Seed Thumbprints. Recipe on page 24.

CARAMEL PILLOWS

These cookies aim to surprise. A delicious, simple shortbread wraps around a caramel candy.

1/2 cup (1 stick) plus 2 tablespoons unsalted
    butter, softened

2/3 cup sugar

1 large egg white

1 teaspoon vanilla extract

1-3/4 cups all-purpose flour

21 chewy caramel candies, unwrapped and cut
    in half

Adjust rack to lower third of oven and preheat oven to 350°F. Using an electric mixer on medium-low speed, cream butter in a large bowl until smooth. Increase mixer speed to medium, add sugar, and mix until well combined and slightly fluffy. Lower mixer speed and add egg white and vanilla, then the flour in two additions, scraping down the sides and mixing until thoroughly combined.

Using 2 level teaspoonfuls of dough, form a flat disk in the palm of your hand. Center a caramel half on the dough and bring the dough up to cover it completely. Roll gently in hands to form a ball. Place balls 1 inch apart onto parchment-lined baking sheets. Bake for 8 to 10 minutes, or until cookies are set and no longer shiny but dull, and the bottoms are browned. Place baking sheets onto a wire rack and allow to cool completely before lifting cookies from parchment paper.

Makes about 3-1/2 dozen.

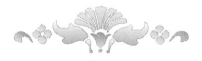

GRANDMA'S OLD-FASHIONED OATMEAL-RAISIN COOKIES

A favorite with mothers of all generations.

1 cup (2 sticks) unsalted butter, at room temperature

1-1/2 cups sugar

1/2 cup packed light-brown sugar

2 large eggs, at room temperature

1 teaspoon vanilla extract

2-1/2 cups all-purpose flour

1 teaspoon baking powder

1 teaspoon baking soda

1/2 teaspoon salt

2 cups uncooked old-fashioned rolled oats

1 cup raisins

In a bowl, cream the butter, gradually adding the sugars, eggs, and vanilla. In a separate bowl, mix the flour, baking powder, baking soda, and salt. Stir the dry ingredients into the creamed mixture until uniformly blended. Stir in the oats and raisins. Cover the dough and refrigerate for at least 2 hours.

Preheat oven to 350°F and grease two large cookie sheets. Using mounded tablespoonfuls of dough, make balls of dough almost 2 inches in diameter and lay them onto the sheets, leaving plenty of room for them to spread. Bake for about 22 minutes, or until lightly browned. Cool the cookies on the sheets for 1 to 2 minutes, then transfer to a rack and cool to room temperature.

Makes about 2 dozen.

ROCK-HARD RAISINS?

❤ Soak them in warm water. Drain and pat dry before using.

DATE OATMEAL COOKIES

Sweet dates and crunchy oats make these a natural for school lunches.

1-3/4 cups all-purpose flour

1 teaspoon baking powder

3/4 teaspoon baking soda

1 teaspoon cinnamon

1/2 teaspoon salt

1 cup (2 sticks) unsalted butter, softened

1 cup sugar

2 large eggs

1 teaspoon vanilla extract

2 cups uncooked quick-cooking rolled oats

1 package (8 ounces) whole pitted dates, coarsely chopped

1 cup chopped walnuts

Sift together flour, baking powder, baking soda, cinnamon, and salt. In a separate bowl, cream the butter and sugar with an electric mixer until light. Beat in the eggs, one at a time. Add vanilla and blend in flour mixture. Beat in oats, dates, and nuts just until thoroughly blended. Shape into 4 logs about 7 inches long. Wrap in plastic and refrigerate until firm.

Adjust rack to lower third of oven and preheat oven to 350°F. Slice each log into 1/8- to 1/4-inch-thick rounds, and place 1 inch apart onto parchment-lined baking sheets. Bake for about 8 minutes, or until cookies are set and light tan on the bottom. Cool on a wire rack.

Makes about 8 dozen.

BUTTERSCOTCH THINS

Eating this cookie will remind you of a favorite childhood snack enjoyed with a tall glass of cold milk. Great with fruit, and with chocolate and caramel ice creams.

2-1/2 cups all-purpose flour

1-1/2 teaspoons cinnamon

1 teaspoon baking soda

1/4 teaspoon salt

1 cup (2 sticks) unsalted butter, softened

1 cup packed light-brown sugar

1 large egg

1 large egg yolk

1 teaspoon vanilla extract

1 cup sliced blanched almonds

Sift together flour, cinnamon, baking soda, and salt. In a separate bowl, cream butter and brown sugar. Add egg and egg yolk, one at a time, then vanilla. Add flour mixture, incorporating thoroughly. Stir in almonds. Shape the soft dough into 4 logs about 7 inches long. Wrap in plastic and refrigerate until firm.

Adjust rack to lower third of oven and preheat oven to 350°F. Slice each log into 1/8-inch-thick rounds, and place 1 inch apart onto parchment-lined baking sheets. Bake for 8 to 10 minutes, or until cookies are set and light tan on the bottom. Cool on a wire rack.

Makes about 9 dozen.

POPPY-SEED THUMBPRINTS

Poppy seeds give these cookies their distinctive crunch. (See photo, page 20.)

2-1/4 cups all-purpose flour

1/4 cup poppy seeds

2/3 cup sugar

1/8 teaspoon salt

1 cup (2 sticks) unsalted butter, softened

1 large egg

1/4 teaspoon lemon extract

1/2 cup strawberry preserves

Adjust rack to lower third of oven and preheat oven to 350°F. Line baking sheets with baking parchment. Place flour, poppy seeds, sugar, and salt into a food processor, and process just to blend ingredients. Add the butter in pieces, processing with on/off bursts until mixture has the consistency of cornmeal. In a small bowl, whisk the egg and lemon extract. With the processor motor running, pour egg mixture down the feed tube, and process just until ingredients form a ball.

Measuring 1 level teaspoonful at a time, shape dough into balls and set 1/2 inch apart onto the baking sheets. Gently make an indentation in the center of each ball, pressing your thumb down almost to the bottom without breaking through the dough. Bake for 10 minutes, or until the cookies are ivory-colored on top and pale golden on the bottom. Transfer cookies to a wire rack to cool. Place 1/4 teaspoonful of strawberry preserves into each indentation.

Makes about 6 dozen.

FULL-CIRCLE COOKIES

These cookies are a simpler version of traditional pretzel-shaped ones. After tasting the buttery cookie with its touch of maple, you'll agree that the flavors are natural companions.

1-1/2 cups plus 2 tablespoons all-purpose flour

1/2 cup unsifted confectioners' sugar

1/4 cup sugar

3/4 cup (1-1/2 sticks) unsalted butter, at room
temperature

1 egg, separated

1/2 teaspoon maple extract

1/2 cup pearl or colored sugar, for decoration

Adjust rack to lower third of oven and preheat oven to 300°F. Line baking sheets with baking parchment. Put the flour, confectioners' sugar, and sugar into a food processor, and process just to blend the ingredients. Add butter, egg yolk, and maple extract, and process just until mixture forms a ball.

On a lightly floured surface, shape 1 teaspoonful of dough at a time into a pencil-like rope 4 to 5 inches long and 1/4 inch in diameter. Form dough ropes into "O" shapes and place about 1 inch apart onto the baking sheets. Lightly beat egg white and brush it onto the cookies. Sprinkle cookies with decorative sugar. Bake for 12 to 15 minutes, or until firm when lightly touched, ivory-colored on top, and pale golden on the bottom. Place baking sheets onto a wire rack to cool before removing cookies.

Makes 7 dozen.

MORE, PLEASE!

❤ Double the recipe or make a second batch before cleaning your equipment.

CHOCOLATE PEANUT-BUTTER COOKIES

These are guaranteed to cure the back-to-school blues, at least for the moment.

6 ounces semisweet chocolate

1/2 cup (1 stick) unsalted butter, softened

2/3 cup salted crunchy natural peanut butter

1 cup packed light-brown sugar

1 large egg, at room temperature

1 teaspoon vanilla extract

2 cups all-purpose flour

1 tablespoon unsweetened cocoa powder

1 teaspoon baking soda

1/4 teaspoon salt

Coarsely chop 2 ounces of the chocolate and put it into the top of a double boiler. Melt the chocolate over, barely simmering water, whisking to smooth. Remove from the heat and cool to room temperature. Preheat oven to 350°F.

Using an electric mixer, cream the butter, peanut butter, and brown sugar until smooth and fluffy. Beat in the egg until smooth, then the vanilla. Sift the dry ingredients into a small bowl and set aside.

Blend the melted chocolate into the creamed mixture. Stir in the dry ingredients, about one-third at a time. Coarsely chop the remaining 4 ounces of chocolate and stir it into the dough.

Using floured hands, roll the dough into 1-1/2-inch balls and place them onto greased baking sheets. Bake for 15 to 17 minutes. When done, the tops of the cookies will be cracked and will feel soft to gentle finger pressure. Cool briefly on the sheets, then transfer to a rack to cool.

Makes about 2 dozen.

HOW DOES YOUR COOKIE CRUMBLE?

♥ **Do you like a soft molasses cookie? Then underbake slightly. Crisp? Overbake slightly.**

MOLASSES CRISPS

Bring back memories or create new ones with these cinnamon-scented favorites.

2 cups all-purpose flour

1-1/2 teaspoons baking soda

1 teaspoon cinnamon

1 teaspoon ginger

1/2 teaspoon cloves

1/4 teaspoon salt

3/4 cup (1-1/2 sticks) unsalted butter, at room temperature

1 cup packed light-brown sugar

1 large egg

1/4 cup light molasses

1/2 cup sugar

Sift flour, baking soda, spices, and salt onto a sheet of waxed paper; set aside. Using an electric mixer at medium-low speed, cream the butter for about 1 minute until smooth. Beat in the brown sugar at medium speed until creamy. Add egg and beat just until fluffy. Add molasses gradually, beating until incorporated. Lower speed and gradually blend in the dry ingredients that were set aside, mixing just until combined. Refrigerate dough for about 1 hour.

Preheat oven to 350°F. Shape dough into small balls about 1-1/4 inches in diameter. Roll dough balls in sugar to coat, and place them 1 inch apart on parchment-lined baking sheets. With a cool baking sheet, press down on cookies to flatten them slightly.

Bake, one sheet at a time, for 8 minutes, or until cookies are flat, feel slightly firm, and are cinnamon-brown. Place baking sheet onto a wire rack and allow cookies to cool before removing from parchment paper.

Makes about 6 dozen.

SNOWBALL COOKIES

These tender "snowballs" have a delicate crunch from the addition of cornmeal. They're perfect with a cup of tea or hot chocolate when you come in from making snowmen!

3/4 cup (1-1/2 sticks) unsalted butter, softened

1/4 cup unsifted confectioners' sugar

1/3 cup sugar

1 teaspoon vanilla extract

1/3 cup yellow cornmeal

1-3/4 cups all-purpose flour

1/4 teaspoon salt

confectioners' sugar, for finishing cookies

Adjust rack to lower third of oven and preheat oven to 350°F. Cream the butter, sugars, and vanilla until smooth. In a separate bowl, mix together the cornmeal, flour, and salt. Combine dry ingredients with butter mixture to form a soft dough. Shape into 1-inch balls (using about 1-1/2 teaspoonfuls of dough per cookie), and space about 1-1/2 inches apart on large, parchment-lined baking sheets. Bake for 12 to 15 minutes, or until bottoms are lightly colored. While cookies are still warm on the baking sheets, sprinkle them with confectioners' sugar through a small sieve. When thoroughly cool, dredge them in confectioners' sugar for a second coating.

Makes about 3 dozen.

MEXICAN WEDDING CAKES

These cookies look like snowballs, just like the preceding recipe, but don't be fooled; the taste is completely different.

3/4 cup pecan halves or pieces

1/2 cup confectioners' sugar

1/4 teaspoon salt

1/2 cup (1 stick) cold unsalted butter, cut into
    8 pieces

1/2 teaspoon vanilla extract

1 cup all-purpose flour

extra confectioners' sugar, for dusting the cookies

Put the pecans, confectioners' sugar, and salt into a food processor, and process nuts to a fine meal. Add half the butter and pulse the machine briefly three or four times. Add the rest of the butter and pulse the machine again, until the butter is smooth, adding the vanilla before the machine stops. Add all the flour to the machine and process until the dough is evenly blended; it will gather into a ball on the blade. Scrape the dough into a bowl and refrigerate for 15 minutes.

Roll dough between palms into 1-1/4-inch balls, and place them onto lightly greased baking sheets, leaving 2 inches between each cookie. Refrigerate the cookies for 15 minutes, and preheat oven to 350°F. Bake cookies for 20 minutes, or until the bottom edges begin to brown. Transfer cookies to a rack to cool. When barely warm, roll in confectioners' sugar. Roll again when completely cooled.

Makes about 1-1/2 dozen.

PUMPKIN SPICE COOKIES

Big, round, and light orange—just like the Harvest Moon. Use the cream-cheese filling as a frosting or to make them into Moon Pies for a truly heavenly treat!

1 cup (2 sticks) unsalted butter, softened

3/4 cup sugar

3/4 cup packed light-brown sugar

1 large egg

1 egg yolk

1/2 cup canned pumpkin

1-1/2 teaspoons vanilla extract

1-1/2 cups all-purpose flour

1-1/2 cups whole-wheat flour

1/2 teaspoon baking soda

1/2 teaspoon baking powder

1/2 teaspoon salt

1 teaspoon EACH cinnamon and ginger

1/2 teaspoon EACH nutmeg and cloves

FILLING (OPTIONAL):

8 ounces cream cheese, softened

2/3 cup sugar

1/2 teaspoon vanilla extract

1/4 teaspoon lemon extract

Cream the butter, gradually adding the sugars, whole egg, and egg yolk until light and fluffy. Blend in pumpkin and vanilla. Sift together remaining ingredients and stir them into creamed mixture, a third at a time. Cover dough and chill for 30 minutes.

Using floured hands, roll dough into 1-1/2-inch balls. Place 2 inches apart onto greased cookie sheets. Bake at 350°F for 15 to 18 minutes. When done, cookies will yield slightly to light finger pressure. Cool briefly on sheets, then transfer to a rack.

Beat together filling ingredients until fluffy. When cookies are completely cool, lightly frost the tops, or spread some filling on the flat side of a cookie and press another cookie onto it to make a sandwich.

Makes about 30 single cookies (15 sandwiches).

When the Recipe Calls for Toasted Nuts . . .

. . . HERE'S WHAT TO DO.

Toasting, or roasting, improves the flavor of any nut. It's a snap to do in the oven or on top of the stove. Store toasted nuts in the freezer, tightly sealed in plastic bags.

OVEN METHOD

Preheat oven to 325°F. Spread the nuts on a large baking sheet—they'll toast more evenly if you don't bunch them all together.

Place the sheet into the preheated oven. Most nuts will take 8 to 10 minutes. They'll toast quicker if you use a dark baking sheet, instead of a shiny one, and if they're at room temperature rather than cold. Just to be safe, set a timer. Usually, when you catch

Walnut-and-Orange Biscotti

Take a break! These Italian-style, "twice-baked" cookies are meant to be dunked in your morning cup of coffee.

1-1/2 cups walnuts

2-3/4 cups all-purpose flour

3/4 teaspoon baking powder

1/2 teaspoon salt

1/2 teaspoon crushed fennel seed

3 large eggs, at room temperature

1 cup sugar

1 teaspoon vanilla extract

finely grated zest of 1 large orange

egg wash (1 egg yolk beaten with 1 tablespoon water)

Spread the walnuts onto a baking sheet and toast them in a 325°F oven for about 10 minutes. Slide nuts onto counter to cool, then chop coarsely and set aside.

Mix together the flour, baking powder, salt, and fennel seed; set aside. Beat eggs and sugar on high speed for 5 minutes, or until thick. Blend in vanilla and zest. Stir in the dry ingredients, then stir in nuts. Let the dough rest for 5 minutes.

Turn dough out onto a floured surface and divide in half. Using floured hands, shape into two 3x12-inch rectangles. Place rectangles onto large, greased and floured baking sheets, leaving some room between them. Brush with egg wash and bake for 40 minutes, or until golden. Remove from oven and cool on the baking sheets for 10 minutes. Reduce heat to 275°F.

Slide the rectangles onto a cutting board. With a serrated knife, slice them diagonally, into 1/2-inch-wide pieces. Place the biscotti, standing up, onto baking sheets. Bake for 20 to 25 minutes longer. Cool on a rack before storing in an airtight container.

Makes about 30 cookies.

the first whiff of the nuts toasting, they're done. But if there's something else cooking and you miss the smell, or you're distracted and forget them, you're sunk. Nuts go from perfectly toasted to burned very quickly. Remove them from the oven when they're fragrant and just a shade darker than when they started.

❤ Immediately slide the nuts onto a large platter or another baking sheet. If you leave them on the hot sheet, they might burn. Spread and cool them thoroughly, especially if you'll be chopping the nuts in a food processor. If you don't cool them first, they'll turn pasty.

STOVETOP METHOD

❤ Preheat a large cast-iron skillet over medium heat. Add the nuts and toast them, stirring frequently, for 5 to 6 minutes. The timing will depend on the level of heat and the type of nut. Watch for the change in color as described above.

–Ken Haedrich

CHOCOLATE ICE-CREAM-SANDWICH COOKIES

Slide a slice of your favorite ice cream between a couple of these thin, crisp chocolate wafers. A summer delight!

3/4 cup (1-1/2 sticks) unsalted butter, at room
   temperature

1 cup packed light-brown sugar

1 large egg, at room temperature

1 teaspoon vanilla extract

1 cup all-purpose flour

1/3 cup unsweetened cocoa powder

3/4 teaspoon baking soda

1/4 teaspoon salt

1 or 2 pints premium ice cream

Using an electric mixer, cream the butter, gradually adding the brown sugar. Add the egg, beating until fluffy. Blend in the vanilla.

Sift flour, cocoa, baking soda, and salt into a bowl. Mix the dry ingredients into the creamed in several stages, until the dough is uniformly smooth. Cover the dough and refrigerate for 15 minutes. Preheat oven to 350°F and grease two cookie sheets.

Using floured hands, gently roll dough into 1-1/4-inch balls. Place the balls onto the cookie sheets, leaving about 3-1/2 inches between each one. Bake for 15 minutes. Cool cookies on the sheets for 2 minutes, then transfer to a rack to cool completely.

About 30 minutes before assembling the cookies, remove the ice cream from the freezer and place it into the refrigerator to soften slightly. To make the cookies, slide the ice cream out of the carton (or peel away the cardboard). Slice through the ice cream to make rounds about 3/4 inch thick. (Use a knife rinsed in hot water.) Sandwich the ice cream between two cookies. Serve at once, or place onto baking sheets and freeze until serving.

Makes about 18 cookies (9 sandwiches).

BAKING WITH KIDS

❤ **Here's the secret ingredient: Find the things they're doing right, and praise them for it.**

WINTER ENERGY COOKIES

Wheat germ, whole-wheat flour, raisins, nuts, and chocolate chips take top billing in these jumbo, wholesome, take-me-along (skiing, snowshoeing, skating!) cookies.

1 cup (2 sticks) unsalted butter, at room temperature

1-1/2 cups packed light-brown sugar

1/3 cup molasses

1/3 cup smooth peanut butter

2 large eggs

1-1/2 teaspoons vanilla extract

1-1/2 cups whole-wheat flour

1 cup all-purpose flour

1 cup toasted wheat germ

1-1/2 teaspoons baking soda

1/2 teaspoon salt

1/2 teaspoon cinnamon

2 cups uncooked rolled oats

1 cup raisins

1 cup chocolate chips

1 cup chopped walnuts or peanuts

Cream the butter, brown sugar, molasses, and peanut butter in a large bowl. Blend in the eggs and vanilla. Mix the flours, wheat germ, baking soda, salt, and cinnamon in a separate bowl. Stir the dry ingredients into the creamed mixture until evenly blended. Stir in the oats, raisins, chocolate chips, and nuts. Cover and refrigerate for 1 hour.

Preheat oven to 350°F and lightly grease cookie sheets. Shape dough into balls using 1/4 cup of dough per cookie. Place onto sheets, leaving 3 inches between them. Flatten slightly with a fork. Bake for 15 to 18 minutes. When done, the tops will still be soft to the touch. Cool on the sheets for 5 minutes, then transfer to a rack to cool.

Makes about 2 dozen.

CORNMEAL SNICKERDOODLES

Even if the corn is only knee-high, you can still enjoy these soft cornmeal butter cookies with a tall glass of lemonade. Just like corn, these are best eaten as fresh as possible.

1 cup (2 sticks) unsalted butter, at room temperature

1/3 cup honey

1/3 cup sugar

2 large eggs, at room temperature

finely grated zest of 1 lemon

1/2 teaspoon vanilla extract

1-1/2 cups all-purpose flour

1 cup yellow cornmeal, preferably stone-ground

1 teaspoon baking powder

1/2 teaspoon salt

extra sugar, to roll cookies in

Cream the butter, honey, and sugar in a large bowl. Beat in the eggs. Stir in the zest and vanilla. In a separate bowl, mix together the flour, cornmeal, baking powder, and salt. Stir the dry ingredients into the creamed mixture in two stages, until evenly blended. Cover and refrigerate the dough for 3 hours. (Dough may be refrigerated overnight.)

Preheat oven to 375°F and grease two large cookie sheets. Shape the dough into 1-1/4-inch balls. Roll the balls in sugar and place them onto the sheets about 2 inches apart. Bake for 15 minutes, or until the tops are slightly resistant to gentle finger pressure. Cool on a rack. Excellent warm, too!

Makes 2 dozen.

Strawberry Blossoms

April showers bring May flowers—and these buttery strawberry blossoms are among our favorites.

1 cup (2 sticks) unsalted butter, at room temperature

1 cup confectioners' sugar

1 teaspoon vanilla extract

1-1/2 cups all-purpose flour

1 cup blanched almonds, processed to a fine meal

1/8 teaspoon salt

1/8 teaspoon baking soda

1/4 cup strawberry preserves

Cream the butter and confectioners' sugar. Blend in the vanilla. In a separate bowl, mix together the flour, almonds, salt, and baking soda. Stir the dry ingredients into the creamed mixture in two stages. Cover the dough and refrigerate for 1 hour.

Roll small pieces of dough into 3/4-inch balls. Arrange 5 balls in a circle, just touching, on ungreased cookie sheets, leaving only enough room in the center for a pinky to fit through. Repeat for the rest of the dough, leaving about 3 inches between each cookie. Refrigerate the sheets for 30 minutes. Preheat oven to 350°F.

Bake the cookies for 20 minutes, or until the bottom edges begin to brown. Cool on the sheets for 1 minute, then transfer to a rack to cool. Spoon about 1/2 teaspoonful of strawberry preserves into the center of each cookie before serving.

Makes about 20 cookies.

HINT

❤ For a professional touch, use smooth preserves piped onto each cookie with a pastry bag.

RASPBERRY CHOCOLATE CRESCENTS

Preserve a batch of summer raspberries for these soft, filled half-moon cookies. (Store-bought preserves are just fine, too.)

1/2 cup (1 stick) unsalted butter, softened

3 ounces cream cheese, softened

2 tablespoons confectioners' sugar

1/4 teaspoon vanilla extract

1 cup plus 3 tablespoons all-purpose flour

1/8 teaspoon salt

1/4 cup raspberry preserves

1/3 cup chocolate chips

extra confectioners' sugar

Cream the butter, cream cheese, and confectioners' sugar. Blend in vanilla. Combine flour and salt, then stir it into creamed mixture. Turn dough out onto a lightly floured surface and knead twice. Flatten dough to about 3/4 inch thick onto a sheet of plastic wrap. Seal and refrigerate for 2 hours.

Roll the dough about 1/8 inch thick on a sheet of lightly floured waxed paper. Cut the dough into 3-inch circles. Put a scant teaspoonful of preserves and 4 or 5 chocolate chips into the center of each circle. Lightly moisten the perimeter of each cookie with a fingertip dipped in water. Fold each cookie in half, pressing the edges to seal. Place the cookies onto lightly greased cookie sheets, crimping the edges with a fork.

Refrigerate for 15 minutes. Preheat oven to 325°F. (Press together scraps, then flatten and refrigerate for 30 minutes before rolling and filling.)

Bake cookies for 22 minutes. Cool for 2 minutes on sheets, then transfer to a rack. When cookies have cooled, dredge in confectioners' sugar.

Makes about 20 cookies.

GINGERSNAPS

These cookies are nicely spicy, with the classic crinkly top and just the right amount of "snap."

3/4 cup (1-1/2 sticks) butter

2 cups sugar

2 eggs, beaten

1/2 cup molasses

2 teaspoons vinegar

3-3/4 cups all-purpose flour

1-1/2 teaspoons baking soda

3 teaspoons ginger

1 teaspoon cinnamon

1/2 teaspoon cloves

Cream together the butter and sugar. Stir in eggs, molasses, and vinegar. Combine dry ingredients and add, mixing well. Form dough into 3/4-inch balls. Bake on ungreased cookie sheets at 325°F for about 12 minutes.

Makes about 10 dozen.

LEMON SUGAR COOKIES

This recipe originally came from a newspaper clipping now yellowed with age. The cookies are delicate and delicious.

2-3/4 cups all-purpose flour

2 teaspoons baking powder

1/4 teaspoon salt

1 cup (2 sticks) butter

2 cups sugar

2 eggs

2 teaspoons lemon zest

3 tablespoons lemon juice

1 cup uncooked quick-cooking rolled oats

Stir together the flour, baking powder, and salt. In a large bowl, cream the butter and sugar. Add eggs, beating well. Beat in the zest and juice. Gradually add flour mixture, then stir in oats. Chill dough thoroughly (for at least 2 hours). Roll level tablespoonfuls of dough into balls and place onto greased cookie sheets, allowing room for cookies to spread. Using a flat-bottomed glass or custard cup that has been greased and dipped in sugar, flatten each ball to a 1/4-inch thickness (dip the glass in sugar each time). Bake at 375°F for 8 to 10 minutes, or until lightly browned around the edges. Cool for 1 minute, then carefully remove from cookie sheets and cool on racks.

Makes 4 dozen.

APRICOT WALNUT CRESCENTS

These rich, delicate, apricot-filled cookies are in the tradition of rugelach and other rolled-up pastries.

2 cups all-purpose flour

dash of salt

1 teaspoon sugar

1 cup (2 sticks) butter

1 cup sour cream

1 egg, lightly beaten

6 tablespoons apricot preserves

6 tablespoons ground walnuts

confectioners' sugar

Mix flour, salt, and sugar. With a pastry blender, cut butter into flour until mixture resembles coarse crumbs. Stir in sour cream and egg. Knead lightly until mixture holds together. Wrap well in plastic wrap and refrigerate for 4 hours or overnight.

Divide dough into thirds. On a lightly floured pastry cloth, roll each third into a circle 11 inches in diameter. Spread each circle evenly with 2 tablespoons apricot preserves and 2 tablespoons ground walnuts. Cut each circle into 12 pie-shaped wedges. Roll up each wedge, starting at the wide end. Place seam side down, about 2 inches apart, onto greased cookie sheets. Bake at 375°F for 20 minutes, or until golden brown. Place onto wire rack to cool. Dust with confectioners' sugar when completely cool.

Makes 3 dozen.

CHOCOLATE BUTTER SWEETS

This is an old southern recipe that migrated north to New England, where it was part of a holiday gift-giving class.
These cookies are delicious in any part of the country, at any time of year!

DOUGH:

1/2 cup (1 stick) butter

1/2 cup confectioners' sugar

1/4 teaspoon salt

1 teaspoon vanilla extract

1-1/4 cups sifted all-purpose flour

1/4 teaspoon baking powder

FILLING:

3 ounces cream cheese, softened

1 cup confectioners' sugar

2 tablespoons all-purpose flour

1 teaspoon vanilla extract

1/2 cup coconut

1/2 cup chopped pecans

FROSTING:

1/2 cup chocolate chips

2 tablespoons butter

2 tablespoons water

3/4 cup confectioners' sugar

For dough: Cream butter and confectioners' sugar. Add salt and vanilla. Mix well. Add flour and baking powder gradually. Roll into 3/4-inch balls. Place onto lightly greased cookie sheets, and flatten with the bottom of a glass dipped in sugar (dip the glass in sugar each time). Bake at 350°F for 10 to 12 minutes.

For filling: While cookies are baking, combine cream cheese, confectioners' sugar, flour, and vanilla. Mix well. Stir in coconut and pecans. Place 1 teaspoonful on top of each warm cookie.

For frosting: Heat chocolate chips, butter, and water over low heat until chocolate melts. Add confectioners' sugar and beat until smooth. Cool slightly. Drizzle a small amount of frosting over each cookie.

Makes about 30 cookies.

NOT TOO SOFT . . .

Butter is soft enough to cream when your finger leaves a dent but the butter still feels cool.

BROWN-SUGAR REFRIGERATOR COOKIES

You can bake one roll and freeze the other, if you prefer. (Wrap the roll securely in plastic wrap or foil for freezing.)
The nutmeg in these cookies makes them special.

1/2 cup (1 stick) butter

1/2 cup margarine

2 cups packed brown sugar

2 eggs

3 cups all-purpose flour

1/2 teaspoon baking soda

1 teaspoon cream of tartar

1/2 teaspoon freshly grated nutmeg

1 tablespoon water

1 teaspoon vanilla extract

Cream butter, margarine, and brown sugar until fluffy. Add eggs and beat well. Combine dry ingredients and add to butter mixture. Add water and vanilla, and mix. Divide dough into two rolls, and wrap each in waxed paper. Chill for several hours or overnight.

Slice 1/4 inch thick, and place 2 inches apart onto ungreased cookie sheets. Bake at 350°F for 10 to 12 minutes, or until golden brown.

Makes about 4-1/2 dozen.

BUTTERSCOTCH ICEBOX COOKIES

You can double this recipe, make two cookie logs, and keep one in the freezer for slice-and-bake cookies on demand.

1/2 cup (1 stick) butter, softened

1-1/4 cups packed brown sugar

1 egg, beaten

1 teaspoon vanilla extract

1-1/4 to 1-3/4 cups all-purpose flour

1/4 teaspoon salt

1-1/2 teaspoons baking powder

1/2 cup chopped nuts

Cream together butter and brown sugar until light. Add egg and vanilla, and mix well. Stir together flour, salt, and baking powder and add to dough, mixing well. Stir in nuts. Form dough into a 2-inch-diameter log and wrap in foil or waxed paper. Chill for 12 to 24 hours. Slice and bake on ungreased cookie sheets at 400°F for 8 to 10 minutes.

Makes about 5 dozen.

ALMOND BISCOTTI

These were made to be dunked into steaming mugs of your favorite java. Try them at home, or pack them along to your favorite ice-skating spot or for an afternoon of skiing.

2 cups whole toasted almonds

3/4 cup packed brown sugar

1-1/2 cups all-purpose flour

1/2 teaspoon baking powder

1/2 teaspoon salt

1/2 teaspoon cinnamon

5 tablespoons cold unsalted butter, cut into pieces

2 large eggs

1 teaspoon vanilla extract

1/2 cup confectioners' sugar, to roll dough in

Preheat oven to 350°F. Put the almonds and brown sugar into a food processor. Chop to a fine meal. Transfer to a bowl. Put flour, baking powder, salt, and cinnamon into processor. Process for several seconds. Add butter and process again to make a fine meal. Mix into the ground nuts. Beat eggs just to liquefy; stir in the vanilla. Mix liquid into dry ingredients by hand until dough packs together.

Divide dough in half. Roll each half in confectioners' sugar into a 2-inch-thick log. Lift each log onto greased cookie sheets and flatten slightly. Bake for 35 minutes. Turn oven down to 300°F. Cool logs for 10 minutes on sheets, then slide them onto a cutting board. Slice logs on the diagonal, about 1/2 inch thick. Place the slices back onto the sheets, standing on their original bottoms. Bake for 30 minutes longer. Cool on a rack.

Makes about 2 dozen.

HINT

♥ For a wholesome version of most any cookie recipe, replace up to half the flour with whole-wheat flour. Cookies will be slightly chewier and denser.

TRIPLE-CHOCOLATE NUT COOKIES

These cookies give a full measure of chocolate, bite-for-bite; sure to delight any chocoholic.

4 ounces semisweet chocolate

1 cup (2 sticks) unsalted butter, at room temperature

3/4 cup packed light-brown sugar

3/4 cup sugar

2 large eggs

1 teaspoon vanilla extract

2-1/4 cups all-purpose flour

1/4 cup unsweetened cocoa powder

1 teaspoon baking soda

1/2 teaspoon salt

1-1/2 cups chopped toasted walnuts or pecans

1 cup chocolate chips

Melt the semisweet chocolate in the top of a double boiler over hot water. Smooth with a whisk and remove from heat. (Chocolate can also be melted in a microwave oven for 1 to 1-1/2 minutes, or until smooth when stirred.) Cream the butter, gradually adding the sugars. Beat in the eggs one at a time, then the vanilla. Fold in the melted chocolate. Sift flour, cocoa, baking soda, and salt, and stir into the creamed ingredients. Fold in the nuts and chocolate chips. Cover and refrigerate the dough for 20 minutes.

Preheat oven to 350°F. Roll the dough into 1-1/2-inch balls and place onto greased cookie sheets, leaving room between them. Bake for 15 minutes. Cool briefly on sheets, then transfer cookies to a rack to cool.

Makes about 3 dozen.

CHOCOLATE CASHEW DELIGHTS

This nutty cashew cookie is topped with a chocolate candy. Look for cashew butter at your local health-food store.

3/4 cup cashew butter

1/2 cup (1 stick) unsalted butter, softened

1-1/4 cups packed light-brown sugar

1 large egg

1 teaspoon vanilla extract

1-1/2 cups all-purpose flour

1 teaspoon baking soda

1/4 teaspoon salt

1 cup chopped roasted cashews

about 30 foil-wrapped chocolate candies

Preheat oven to 350°F and grease two cookie sheets. Cream the cashew butter, butter, and brown sugar. Beat in the egg and vanilla until smooth. Sift flour, baking soda, and salt, and stir into the creamed mixture. Fold in the chopped cashews. Unwrap the chocolates. With floured hands, roll the dough into 1-1/2-inch balls, leaving room between them on the sheets. Bake for 15 to 17 minutes, or until the tops are gently rounded and still soft to the touch. As the cookies come out of the oven, firmly press a chocolate candy into the center of each one. Cool on the sheets for 5 minutes, then transfer to a rack to cool.

Makes about 2-1/2 dozen.

MOLASSES SPICE COOKIES

These cookies make a great after-school snack or lunch-box treat.

1/2 cup (1 stick) unsalted butter, softened

2/3 cup packed light-brown sugar

1/2 cup molasses

1 large egg

1 teaspoon vanilla extract

2 cups all-purpose flour

1 teaspoon baking soda

1/4 teaspoon salt

2 teaspoons ground ginger

1/2 teaspoon cinnamon

1/2 teaspoon ground cardamom

Cream the butter, brown sugar, and molasses. Beat in the egg and vanilla. Sift remaining ingredients and stir them into the creamed mixture. Cover and refrigerate the dough for at least 1 hour. Preheat oven to 350°F. Roll the dough into 1-1/2-inch balls and place them onto greased baking sheets, leaving some room between them. Bake for 16 to 18 minutes. Cool briefly on the sheets, then transfer cookies to a rack to cool.

Makes about 2-1/2 dozen.

LIGHT LEMON SHORTBREAD COOKIES

Fragrant and delicate, these cookies are the perfect partner to a bowl of fresh summer berries and cream.

1 cup (2 sticks) unsalted butter, softened

1-1/2 teaspoons lemon extract

1 teaspoon vanilla extract

finely grated zest of 2 lemons

2-1/4 cups all-purpose flour

2/3 cup confectioners' sugar

2 tablespoons cornstarch

1/4 teaspoon salt

extra confectioners' sugar, for dusting cooled cookies

Cream the butter, lemon extract, vanilla, and zest. Sift the remaining ingredients (except the extra confectioners' sugar), and gradually stir them into the butter mixture until you have a firm dough. Divide the dough in half. Roll each half into a cylinder 9 inches long, and wrap each in a piece of waxed paper. Refrigerate for at least 2 hours or overnight.

Preheat oven to 325°F. Cut dough into slices 1/3 inch thick. Lay slices onto ungreased baking sheets, leaving a little room between them; they barely spread. Bake for 22 minutes. Cool on the sheets for 1 minute or so, then transfer cookies to a rack to cool. When thoroughly cool, dust them with confectioners' sugar.

Makes about 3 dozen.

HINT

💜 Most cookie doughs freeze well for up to a month. Thaw overnight in the fridge.

BLUEBERRY SPIRALS

These cookies are beautiful as well as delicious; the cinnamon gives a nice twist to the blueberry flavor.

1 cup (2 sticks) unsalted butter, at room temperature

1/4 pound cream cheese, softened

1 teaspoon vanilla extract

finely grated zest of 1 lemon

2 cups all-purpose flour

1/4 cup confectioners' sugar

1/2 teaspoon salt

3 tablespoons sugar

2 teaspoons cinnamon

9 tablespoons blueberry preserves

a little milk

extra sugar, for sprinkling

Cream butter, cream cheese, vanilla, and zest. Sift flour, confectioners' sugar, and salt. Gradually stir into creamed mixture. Divide dough into thirds and flatten into 3/4-inch-thick disks. Wrap and refrigerate for at least 1 hour. Mix sugar with cinnamon and set aside.

Roll one piece of dough into a 12-inch circle on floured waxed paper. Slide dough onto a cookie sheet and refrigerate for 10 minutes. Spread 3 tablespoons preserves over dough. Sprinkle generously with cinnamon sugar. Cut into 16 wedges. Roll up wedges, starting at the wide end. Place onto greased cookie sheets, seam down. Refrigerate for 15 minutes. Repeat for other two pieces of dough. Brush spirals with milk and sprinkle with plain sugar. Bake at 350°F for 20 minutes. Cool on a rack.

Makes 4 dozen.

EASY ROLLING

❤ Draw a 12-inch circle on a piece of paper and slip it under the waxed paper to use as a guide.

FROM THE ARCHIVES

How to Pack Cookies for Mailing

from *Good Cooking Made Easy*, Lever Brothers, 1942

How our boys enjoy cookies from home! Cookies fragrant with spices; cookies rich with chocolate, nuts, or fruits! Send a box of cookies to a serviceman today!

Pack cookies into a sturdy cardboard box or a big empty Spry can. Line box with waxed paper and put a piece of cardboard between layers. Fill empty spaces with crumpled waxed paper. Bar cookies can be mailed in the pans they are baked in. Wrap box in heavy paper, tie securely, and address plainly.

CANTEEN COOKIE BARS

1/2 cup shortening	2 eggs, beaten
1/4 teaspoon salt	2 tablespoons flour
1-1/2 cups packed brown sugar, divided	1/2 teaspoon baking powder
1 cup sifted flour	1-1/2 cups shredded coconut
1 teaspoon vanilla extract	1 cup nuts, coarsely chopped

Preheat oven to 325°F. Combine shortening and salt. Add 1/2 cup of the brown sugar and cream well. Add the 1 cup flour and blend. Spread in a greased 12x8-inch pan. Bake for 20 minutes, or until firm and golden brown. Add remaining 1 cup brown sugar and the vanilla to the eggs, beating until thick and foamy. Then add the 2 tablespoons flour, baking powder, coconut, and nuts and blend. Spread over baked mixture. Return to oven and bake for 25 minutes. Cool and cut into small bars.

Makes 2 dozen 2-inch bars.

Drop Cookies

❤ Drop cookies are pushed, a rounded teaspoonful at a time, onto a cool cookie sheet. (Many bakers chill the dough and even chill the cookie sheets ahead of time.) Drop cookies usually spread as they bake, so be sure to allow about two inches between mounds of dough.

PHOTO

Sesame Crisps. Recipe on page 48.

MAPLE PECAN DROPS

Here's an easy recipe. It makes a cookie that tastes like candy!

1-1/2 cups all-purpose flour

1/2 teaspoon baking soda

1/4 teaspoon salt

1 cup (2 sticks) unsalted butter, softened

3/4 cup plus 2 tablespoons packed dark-brown sugar

1 large egg

1 teaspoon pure vanilla extract

1/2 teaspoon maple extract

2 cups (8 ounces) chopped pecans

Adjust rack to lower third of oven and preheat oven to 350°F. Line a large cookie sheet with baking parchment.

In a bowl, whisk or stir with a rubber spatula the flour, baking soda, and salt just to combine; set aside. Using an electric mixer, cream the butter with the brown sugar until mixture is creamy. Mix in the egg and extracts. Stir in the flour mixture, then the nuts.

Drop dough by level measuring tablespoonfuls about 1-1/2 inches apart onto the baking sheet. Bake for about 9 minutes, or until cookies are light brown on the bottom and no longer shiny on top.

Makes about 2-1/2 dozen.

HONEY-LACED OATMEAL COOKIES

Wafer thin, hearty, and healthy, an ideal accompaniment to luscious fall apples or pears.

1/4 cup (1/2 stick) unsalted butter

1/4 cup sugar

1/4 cup honey

1/4 cup all-purpose flour

1 teaspoon finely grated orange zest

1/4 teaspoon cinnamon

1/2 cup uncooked old-fashioned rolled oats

Adjust rack to lower third of oven and preheat oven to 350°F. Line cookie sheets with aluminum foil. Melt butter with sugar and honey, blending well. Pour into a bowl and stir in the flour, zest, cinnamon, and oats. Drop batter by measuring teaspoonfuls about 2 inches apart onto baking sheets. Bake for 8 to 10 minutes, or until bubbly and brown. Place baking sheets onto racks to cool. Remove cookies when almost completely cool.

Makes about 2-1/2 dozen.

SUPER-DUPER PEANUT-BUTTER
CHOCOLATE-CHIP COOKIES

Crispy rice cereal gives these sensational cookies an extra crunch. Be sure to include one or two in school lunch boxes.

2-1/3 cups all-purpose flour

1 teaspoon baking soda

1/2 teaspoon baking powder

1/8 teaspoon salt

1 cup (2 sticks) unsalted butter, softened

1 cup packed brown sugar

2/3 cup sugar

1/3 cup creamy peanut butter

2 large eggs

2 teaspoons vanilla extract

1 cup chopped walnuts

1 cup semisweet chocolate chips

1 cup crispy rice cereal

Adjust rack to lower third of oven and preheat oven to 350°F. Sift the flour, baking soda, baking powder, and salt onto a sheet of waxed paper. Using an electric mixer on low speed, cream the butter, sugars, and peanut butter just until thoroughly blended. Mix in the eggs and vanilla until well combined. Add the dry ingredients, then the walnuts and chocolate chips. Using a rubber spatula, lightly stir in the rice cereal by hand so as not to crush the cereal into crumbs.

Drop rounded tablespoonfuls of batter onto parchment-lined baking sheets, about 2 inches apart, and bake for 9 to 11 minutes, or until cookies are golden. (Do not overbake.) Remove cookies from the parchment paper to a wire rack to cool.

Makes about 4 dozen.

COOLER MOVES

♥ Generally speaking, most cookies will benefit from cooling on the baking sheet for 1 or 2 minutes so they can firm up slightly before being transferred to a wire rack.

The World's Best Chocolate-Chip Cookies

When you make America's favorite cookie, the results ought to be splendid.
by Catherine Vodrey

■ It used to be that everyone I knew made a much better chocolate-chip cookie than I did. I got a little tired of it, especially when I'd ask for the recipe and they would shrug and say, "I just used the one on the chocolate-chip package."

I've tried that recipe, and though it *does* make cookies, they aren't outstanding. So I went to work, read everything I could find written by other cooks, and developed the following recipe. It works.

CHEWY CHOCOLATE-CHIP COOKIES

These keep for several days in an airtight container. You can make the dough in advance and freeze it, too. (Chill it in the refrigerator until firm enough to handle, and then form into a log about 12 to 14 inches long. Wrap well in a double thickness of waxed paper, twisting the ends closed, and freeze. Then, when you want cookies, slice off pieces with a sharp knife, adding about 2 minutes to the total baking time.)

1/2 cup (1 stick) unsalted butter

2 cups all-purpose flour

1/2 teaspoon baking soda

1 teaspoon salt

1/2 cup plus 2 tablespoons sugar

1/3 cup plus 2 tablespoons packed brown sugar

1 large egg, plus 1 large egg yolk

2-1/2 teaspoons vanilla extract

1-1/2 cups chocolate chips

Preheat oven to 325°F. Melt the butter over low heat and set aside to cool. Put oven racks at the top and lower-middle positions. Stir together the flour, baking soda, and salt in a small bowl and set aside.

In the large bowl of an electric mixer, on low speed beat together the butter and both sugars until thoroughly blended. Beat in the egg, egg yolk, and vanilla. Add the dry ingredients, and on the lowest mixer speed beat until just combined. Fold in the chocolate chips.

Place large scoops of dough (about 2 tablespoons per scoop) onto parchment-covered cookie sheets, about 8 or 9 scoops per sheet. (If you don't have baking parchment, grease the cookie sheets; the cookies will end up slightly more crispy on the bottoms.)

Place one cookie sheet on each oven rack. Bake for 6 to 8 minutes, then reverse positions of the cookie sheets. Bake for another 6 to 8 minutes, until just barely golden brown and puffed. Remove from the oven and let cool on the cookie sheets for about 10 minutes before removing to wire racks to cool completely. Repeat for remaining cookie dough.

Makes about 2-1/2 dozen.

MIXED-NUT MACAROONS

Fragrant hazelnuts and almonds are perfect partners in these flourless cookies. It's better to underbake rather than overbake them to preserve a moist, chewy center and a nutty flavor.

3/4 cup sugar

4 ounces EACH unblanched almonds and hazelnuts, toasted and ground to yield 2 cups total nut meal

1/3 cup egg whites (from 2 to 3 large eggs)

1 teaspoon vanilla extract

1/8 teaspoon salt

Adjust rack to lower third of oven and preheat oven to 325°F. In a medium bowl, mix the sugar and the nut meal briefly with a wire whisk. Add the egg whites, vanilla, and salt to the dry ingredients, and stir just to blend together.

Drop about 1-1/2 teaspoonfuls of mixture, about 1-1/2 inches apart, onto a baking sheet lined with baking parchment. Using a pastry brush dipped in cold water, pat each mound to flatten slightly. Bake for 13 to 15 minutes, or until the macaroons are light golden. Remove baking sheet from oven. Lift parchment paper with macaroons to a wire rack to cool completely. The warm macaroons will stick to the parchment paper, but when completely cool, they will easily lift off.

Macaroons are best eaten the same day they are baked, but they will keep in an airtight plastic container at room temperature for up to two days.

Makes about 3-1/2 dozen.

ZUCCHINI COOKIES

These delicious cookies use the season's bounty of zucchini.

2 cups all-purpose flour

1 teaspoon baking powder

1/2 teaspoon ground cinnamon

1/4 teaspoon EACH ground nutmeg and cloves

1/2 teaspoon salt

1 cup (2 sticks) unsalted butter, softened

3/4 cup sugar

1 large egg

1 cup shredded, unpeeled zucchini (about 4 ounces)

Adjust rack to lower third of oven and preheat oven to 350°F. Line a cookie sheet with baking parchment.

In a bowl, combine the flour, baking powder, cinnamon, nutmeg, cloves, and salt with a rubber spatula; set aside. In a separate bowl, using an electric mixer, beat butter and sugar until just light. Lower speed and mix in egg. Stir in flour mixture until well blended. Stir in zucchini.

Drop tablespoonfuls of batter onto the baking sheet. Bake for 12 to 14 minutes, or until golden brown.

Makes about 2-1/2 dozen.

SESAME CRISPS

These bake thin and crisp; eat them with fruit sorbets and almost any flavor of ice cream. (See photo, page 42.)

1/2 cup all-purpose flour

1/8 teaspoon salt

1/8 teaspoon baking soda

1/2 cup (1 stick) unsalted butter, softened

1 cup packed light-brown sugar

1 large egg

1/2 cup sesame seeds

Adjust rack to lower third of oven and preheat oven to 325°F. Line baking sheets with baking parchment. Sift together the flour, salt, and baking soda. In a separate bowl, cream the butter with the brown sugar and add the egg, blending well. Stir in the flour mixture and the sesame seeds. Using a 1/2-teaspoon measure, drop batter by rounded spoonfuls about 2 inches apart onto the baking sheets. Bake for 6 to 8 minutes (cookies will puff at first, then flatten and brown). Set baking sheets onto a cooling rack. Cool cookies completely before removing.

Makes about 4-1/2 dozen.

SPICY WALNUT COOKIES

These cookies owe their delicate texture to the combination of baking soda and cream of tartar, a version of homemade baking powder.

2 cups all-purpose flour

1 teaspoon cinnamon

1/2 teaspoon EACH baking soda and cream of tartar

3/4 teaspoon ginger

1/4 teaspoon EACH nutmeg and cloves

1/8 teaspoon salt

1 cup (2 sticks) unsalted butter, softened

1-1/3 cups unsifted confectioners' sugar

1 large egg

1 teaspoon vanilla extract

84 walnut halves

Adjust rack to lower third of oven and preheat oven to 325°F. Line baking sheets with baking parchment. Sift flour with cinnamon, baking soda, cream of tartar, ginger, nutmeg, cloves, and salt. In a separate bowl, beat butter until creamy; gradually add confectioners' sugar, then egg and vanilla, and continue beating until mixture is light. Stir in dry ingredients, incorporating thoroughly.

Using a 1/2-teaspoon measure, drop dough by rounded spoonfuls onto baking sheets and press a walnut half onto each cookie, flattening slightly. Bake for about 10 minutes, or until pale golden on the bottom.

Makes about 7 dozen.

LEMON POPPY-SEED RAINDROPS

Even though we call them raindrops, these simple, lemon-scented cookies are bound to put some sunshine into your day!

1 cup (2 sticks) unsalted butter, at room temperature

3/4 cup sugar

1 large egg, at room temperature

1 teaspoon vanilla extract

1 teaspoon lemon extract

finely grated zest of 1 lemon

1/4 teaspoon salt

2-1/3 cups all-purpose flour

1/3 cup poppy seeds

coarse granulated sugar

Cream the butter in an electric mixer, gradually adding the sugar. Beat the mixture until fluffy, adding the egg, extracts, zest, and salt. Blend in the flour, about half at a time, followed by the poppy seeds. Cover and refrigerate the dough for 15 minutes. Preheat oven to 350°F and get out two large cookie sheets.

Using a well-mounded teaspoonful, spoon the dough onto the ungreased sheets, leaving about 2 inches between each one. Sprinkle each cookie with the course sugar. Bake for 18 to 20 minutes, or until the bottom edges begin to brown. Cool on the sheets for 1 minute, then transfer the cookies to a rack to cool.

Makes about 2-1/2 dozen.

CRUMB COOKIES

Is the cupboard almost bare? Never mind. Pull out a few pantry staples and whip up these incredible crunchy crumb cookies.

5 slices whole-grain bread

6 whole plain graham crackers, broken up

1 cup whole pecans

3/4 cup packed light-brown sugar

1/2 teaspoon cinnamon

1/4 teaspoon ground cloves

1/4 teaspoon salt

1/4 cup (1/2 stick) cold unsalted butter

1 large egg, lightly beaten

1/4 cup all-purpose flour

confectioners' sugar

Put the bread into a warm, dry spot and leave it until crumbly dry. Break into pieces and crush or process to make fine crumbs. Measure 3/4 cup of crumbs into a food processor and add broken graham crackers, pecans, brown sugar, cinnamon, cloves, and salt. Process to make a fine meal. Cut butter into pieces and process with meal until uniformly dampened and slightly clumpy. Preheat oven to 350°F and grease one large cookie sheet.

Transfer crumb mixture to a bowl and drizzle egg over it. Mix with your hands until evenly blended. Add flour and mix again. To shape cookies, pack dough into a deep tablespoon measure, leveling the top. Pressing on one side of the cookie, carefully push it out of the spoon. Dredge cookie in confectioners' sugar and lay it flat side down onto the sheet. Repeat for the rest of the dough, leaving 1 inch between cookies. Bake for 15 minutes, or until surface is semifirm to the touch. Cool cookies briefly on the sheet, then transfer to a rack to cool.

Makes about 2 dozen.

PUMPKIN AND FRESH-GINGER COOKIES

These soft, cakey cookies are best eaten the same day they're baked. That won't be any trouble!

1-1/4 cups packed light-brown sugar

1 cup pumpkin puree

1 large egg

2 tablespoons grated fresh gingerroot, or more to taste

2 tablespoons sour cream

1 teaspoon vanilla extract

1/2 cup (1 stick) unsalted butter, softened

2-1/4 cups all-purpose flour

1 teaspoon baking soda

1 teaspoon baking powder

1/2 teaspoon salt

1/2 teaspoon cinnamon

1 cup chopped walnuts

1 cup currants or chopped raisins

Preheat oven to 350°F and lightly grease two cookie sheets. Combine brown sugar, pumpkin, egg, gingerroot, sour cream, and vanilla in a food processor. Process to a smooth puree. Add the soft butter and process for 8 more seconds.

In a separate bowl, mix the flour, baking soda, baking powder, salt, and cinnamon. Stir the dry ingredients into the liquid in two stages, just until blended. Fold in the walnuts and currants (or raisins). Spoon heaping tablespoonfuls of dough onto the baking sheets, leaving 2-1/2 inches between each one. Bake for 15 minutes. When done, the cookies will form a crust, but they'll still be soft to the touch. Cool on the sheets for 2 minutes, then transfer to a rack to finish cooling.

Makes about 2 dozen.

SOFTEN UP

❤ It's a classic problem——you're ready to bake, but your butter is rock hard. To soften it quickly, grate the butter onto a plate or cut it into thin pats. Or microwave 1 stick of butter for 10 seconds just to soften——if it melts, it will change the outcome.

CRANBERRY CHOCOLATE-CHIP COOKIES

The tart, dried version of fall's "bouncing bog berry" is the perfect counterpoint to sweet chocolate pieces in this chunky cookie.
Glasses of cold milk are a must!

1 cup (2 sticks) unsalted butter, at room
    temperature

1-1/2 cups packed light-brown sugar

2 large eggs, at room temperature

1 teaspoon vanilla extract

2-1/4 cups all-purpose flour

1/4 teaspoon baking soda

1/4 teaspoon salt

1 cup unsweetened dried cranberries (do not
    substitute fresh berries)

1 cup chopped walnuts

1 cup chocolate chips

Cream the butter in a large bowl, gradually adding the brown sugar. Add the eggs one at a time, beating well after each one. Blend in the vanilla.

Mix together the flour, baking soda, and salt. Stir the dry ingredients into the creamed mixture in two stages. Stir in the cranberries, walnuts, and chocolate chips. Cover the dough and refrigerate for 1 hour.

Line two cookie sheets with foil and preheat oven to 350°F. Spoon heaping tablespoonfuls of dough onto the sheets, leaving 3 inches between each cookie. Bake for about 20 minutes, or until golden brown. Transfer the cookies to a rack to cool.

Makes about 4 dozen.

BEACON HILL COOKIES

This recipe has been passed around among friends and from mothers to daughters for almost 50 years—a testament
to these wonderful cookies.

1 cup (6 ounces) chocolate bits

2 egg whites

dash of salt

1/2 cup sugar

1/2 teaspoon vanilla extract

1/2 teaspoon vinegar

3/4 cup walnuts, coarsely chopped

In a double boiler, melt chocolate bits over simmering water. Meanwhile, beat egg whites with a dash of salt until foamy. Gradually add sugar, beating well until stiff peaks are formed. Beat in vanilla and vinegar. Fold in melted chocolate and walnuts. Drop onto greased cookie sheets, and bake for 10 minutes at 350°F.

Makes 3 dozen.

RANGER COOKIES

We're not sure how these cookies got their name, but they've been a lunch-box favorite since the 1950s.

1 cup (2 sticks) butter

1 cup packed brown sugar

1 cup sugar

2 eggs

1 teaspoon vanilla extract

2 cups all-purpose flour

1 teaspoon baking soda

1 teaspoon baking powder

1/2 teaspoon salt

2 cups uncooked rolled oats

2 cups Rice Krispies or Special K cereal

2 cups coconut

Cream together butter and sugars. Add eggs and vanilla and mix well. Stir together flour, baking soda, baking powder, and salt and add to dough, mixing well. Stir in oats, cereal, and coconut. Drop by rounded spoonfuls onto cookie sheets and bake at 350°F for 8 to 10 minutes.

Makes about 4 dozen.

OATMEAL CHOCOLATE-CHIP COOKIES

The oats and oil (instead of butter) make these cookies deliciously chewy.

1/2 cup oil

1/2 cup packed brown sugar

1/2 cup sugar

1 egg

1 teaspoon vanilla extract

1 tablespoon milk

1 cup all-purpose flour

1/2 teaspoon baking soda

1/2 teaspoon baking powder

pinch of salt

1 cup uncooked rolled oats

1/2 cup chocolate chips

Cream together oil and sugars. Beat in the egg. Add vanilla and milk and mix well. Stir together the dry ingredients and beat into the wet mixture. When smooth, stir in oats and chocolate chips. Drop by tablespoonfuls about 2 inches apart onto ungreased cookie sheets. Bake at 350°F for 10 to 12 minutes—do not overcook.

Makes about 3 dozen.

CHOCOLATE ORANGE DELIGHTS

Frances E. Callahan won third prize in the 1989 Old Farmer's Almanac Holiday Cookies and Bars Recipe Contest with this classic combination of flavors.

3 ounces unsweetened chocolate

3/4 cup (1-1/2 sticks) butter

1 cup packed brown sugar

1 cup sugar

1/2 cup sour cream

2 eggs

2 teaspoons grated orange peel

2 cups all-purpose flour

1 teaspoon baking soda

1/2 teaspoon salt

1 cup chopped walnuts or pecans

2 cups chocolate chips

CHOCOLATE GLAZE:

3 ounces semisweet chocolate

1 teaspoon orange extract

1/4 cup (1/2 stick) butter

Melt unsweetened chocolate and allow to cool. Cream butter and sugars thoroughly until light. Add sour cream, eggs, orange peel, and melted chocolate and beat well. Stir in flour, baking soda, and salt. Add nuts and chocolate chips. Drop dough by rounded teaspoonfuls onto lightly greased baking sheets. Bake for 12 to 15 minutes at 375°F. Let cookies cool on wire racks.

For chocolate glaze: Melt semisweet chocolate with extract in a small, heavy saucepan over low heat. Add butter a tablespoon at a time. Stir until smooth. Spread onto cookies; if desired, decorate with candy sprinkles before glaze sets.

Makes about 6 dozen.

MELT, DON'T SEIZE

Chocolate must be melted slowly over low heat or it will "seize"——become stiff and pasty——rather than smooth and silky.

Cutout Cookies

❤ Also called rolled cookies, these are made from dough that is chilled briefly (about 20 minutes) and divided into two or three portions that are easy to work with. Scraps from rolling can be gathered, chilled, and rerolled, although the cookies cut from the scraps will not be quite as tender as those from the initial rolling.

PHOTO

Toffee Kisses. Recipe on page 56.

TOFFEE KISSES

Here are kisses you'll savor for a long time. (See photo, page 54.)

1 cup plus 2 tablespoons all-purpose flour

2 tablespoons cornstarch

1/8 teaspoon salt

1/2 cup (1 stick) unsalted butter, cut into
 1/4-inch pieces

1/4 cup sugar

1 teaspoon vanilla extract

1/3 cup English toffee bits or almond brickle
 chips

Sift flour, cornstarch, and salt onto a sheet of waxed paper; set aside. In a large bowl, beat the butter and sugar with an electric mixer on medium speed. Beat in the vanilla. Stir in the flour mixture, then the toffee bits (or almond chips), blending well.

Transfer to a work surface. Divide dough in half and roll each half between sheets of waxed paper into a circle 1/8 inch thick. Chill the disks for about 2 hours, or until firm.

Adjust rack to lower third of oven and preheat oven to 325°F. Peel off the top sheet of waxed paper from one dough disk. Cut out cookies using a 2-inch lip-shaped cutter. Place 1/2 inch apart onto large baking sheets lined with baking parchment. Bake for 10 to 12 minutes, or until pale brown on the bottom. Cool on wire racks. Repeat for remaining chilled dough disk.

Makes 2-1/2 dozen.

WHITE-CHOCOLATE SPICE COOKIES

This spicy ginger cookie is tamed with a creamy topping.

1-1/2 cups unsifted all-purpose flour

1/2 cup unsifted whole-wheat flour

2/3 cup packed brown sugar

3/4 teaspoon EACH ground ginger, cinnamon, and
 allspice

1 cup (2 sticks) unsalted butter, softened and cut
 into slices

1 tablespoon water

1 teaspoon vanilla extract

TOPPING:

5 ounces pure white chocolate, finely chopped
 (not chips)

2 tablespoons vegetable shortening

Mix together flours, sugar, and spices. Cut in butter until consistency of cornmeal. Combine water and vanilla, add to flour mixture, and stir until dough forms a ball. Divide dough in half. Roll each half between sheets of waxed paper until 1/4 inch thick. Chill for about 1 hour, or until firm.

Preheat oven to 325°F. Working with one piece of chilled dough at a time, cut out cookies using a 1-1/2-inch-round cutter. Space 1/2 inch apart on parchment-lined baking sheets. Bake cookies for about 15 minutes, or until pale brown on bottoms. Cool on wire racks. Repeat for remaining dough.

■ For topping: Fill bottom of a double boiler with 1 inch of hot water. In top pan, combine white chocolate and shortening, stirring until smooth. Dip each cookie halfway into chocolate, then place onto waxed paper. With a fork dipped into the chocolate, flick streaks over cookies. Chill for about 10 minutes, or just until chocolate sets.

Makes about 6 dozen.

UNEVEN HEAT

❤ All ovens have "hot spots," so to ensure even browning, rotate the cookie sheet halfway through the baking time.

HAPPY-HEART COOKIES

You'll start a happy conversation when you give these cookies to your valentine.

2-1/2 cups all-purpose flour

2/3 cup sugar

1/2 teaspoon ground cardamom

1/4 teaspoon salt

1 cup (2 sticks) unsalted butter, at room temperature
and cut into 1/2-inch slices

1 teaspoon vanilla extract

2 teaspoons finely grated orange zest

1/4 cup jam, such as orange marmalade or apricot

candy conversation hearts

Stir together flour, sugar, cardamom, and salt. Cut in butter with a pastry blender until dough has the consistency of cornmeal. Add vanilla and zest, and stir until dough forms a ball.

Divide dough in half. Roll each half between sheets of waxed paper into a circle 1/8 inch thick. Chill circles for about 2 hours, or until firm.

Preheat oven to 325°F. Peel off top sheet of paper from one dough circle and cut out cookies using a 2-inch heart-shaped cutter. Place 1/2 inch apart on baking sheets lined with baking parchment. Bake cookies for 15 to 20 minutes, or until pale brown on bottoms. Cool on wire racks. Repeat for remaining dough.

To "glue" a piece of candy onto each cookie, simmer jam in a small pan to thicken, stirring occasionally. Let cool until warm to touch. Spoon a tiny dot onto upper-right portion of each cookie, and gently press a candy conversation heart on top. (You should not see jam.)

Makes about 3-1/2 dozen.

SAND DOLLARS

These look like the real thing, but they taste a lot better: thin, crisp, and sweet.

1/2 cup (1 stick) unsalted butter, at room temperature

3/4 cup sugar, plus a little extra to sprinkle on top

1 egg yolk

1 teaspoon vanilla extract

1-1/4 cups all-purpose flour

1/4 teaspoon salt

1 egg white, lightly beaten

thinly sliced blanched almonds, for decoration

Cream the butter, gradually beating in the sugar, egg yolk, and vanilla. Mix the flour and salt, slowly stirring the dry ingredients into the creamed. Gather the dough into a ball, then flatten it onto a large sheet of plastic wrap. Wrap the dough, slip it into a plastic bag, and refrigerate for at least 4 hours, or until firm.

When the dough is thoroughly chilled, let it sit at room temperature for about 15 minutes, or until it can be rolled. Preheat oven to 350°F and lightly grease two large cookie sheets.

Roll the dough about 1/8 inch thick on a sheet of waxed paper or plastic wrap. Cut dough into 2- or 2-1/4-inch rounds and place them onto the sheets, leaving about 1-1/2 inches between each one. (Gather the scraps and reroll them, too.) Brush cookies lightly with egg white, then arrange 5 almond slices on each cookie, like the spokes of a wheel. Brush again with egg white, very lightly, then sprinkle each one with a little sugar. Bake for 10 to 12 minutes; they should start to brown, especially around the edges. Briefly cool the cookies on the sheets, then transfer to a rack and finish cooling.

Makes about 2 dozen.

TIMELY ADVICE

❤ Baking time can vary greatly from one oven to another. Always check your bars or cookies before the time is up.

CINNAMON STARS

For a pretty holiday decoration, poke a small hole in these before baking and hang them from your tree with a thin ribbon.

1 cup (2 sticks) unsalted butter, softened

3/4 cup sugar

2 egg yolks

1-1/2 teaspoons vanilla extract

finely grated zest of 1 orange

2-2/3 cups all-purpose flour

1 teaspoon cinnamon

1/4 teaspoon salt

FROSTING:

1 cup confectioners' sugar

4 to 5 teaspoons milk

1 teaspoon butter, softened

1 or 2 drops vanilla extract

colored sugars, for decoration

Using an electric mixer, cream the butter, gradually adding the sugar. Blend in yolks and beat until fluffy. Blend in vanilla and zest.

Sift remaining dry ingredients into a bowl and stir them into the creamed mixture in several stages, until the dough is uniform. Gather dough into a ball and flatten on a large piece of plastic wrap to about 3/4 inch thick. Wrap the dough, then slide it into a plastic bag. Seal and refrigerate overnight.

Preheat oven to 325°F and grease two large cookie sheets. On a lightly floured sheet of waxed paper, roll the dough slightly less than 1/4 inch thick. Cut into star shapes with a cookie cutter and place onto sheets, leaving a little room between them. Bake for 13 to 15 minutes. Cool on a rack.

For frosting: Combine confectioners' sugar and 4 teaspoons of the milk in a small bowl. Whisk to smooth, adding the butter and vanilla. It should be thick but spreadable. Use more drops of milk, if necessary. Spread frosting over the cookies, then sprinkle with colored sugar.

Makes about 2 dozen.

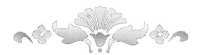

COOL TIP

Warm baking sheets can cause cookies to flatten and spread, so allow sheets to cool between batches.

GRANNY'S ROLLED COOKIES

From Valentine hearts to Christmas trees, these cookies make any holiday special with their chocolate flourish.

1/2 cup (1 stick) unsalted butter, at room
    temperature

1 cup sugar

1 large egg, at room temperature

2 teaspoons vanilla extract

1 tablespoon milk

2 cups all-purpose flour

1 teaspoon baking powder

1/4 teaspoon salt

confectioners' sugar, for dusting the cookies

2 ounces semisweet chocolate, coarsely chopped

Cream the butter, sugar, and egg until soft and creamy. Beat in the vanilla and milk. Mix the flour, baking powder, and salt. Stir the dry mixture into the creamed ingredients to make a uniform dough. Knead several times in the bowl, then flatten the dough to 3/4 inch thick on a piece of waxed paper. Wrap in plastic and refrigerate for 2 hours.

Roll the dough 1/3 inch thick on lightly floured waxed paper. Cut out with a cookie cutter. Place cookies 1 inch apart onto lightly greased cookie sheets. Refrigerate for 15 minutes. Preheat oven to 350°F.

Bake for 12 to 15 minutes, or until the edges just begin to brown. Transfer cookies to a rack to cool. Dust them with confectioners' sugar while still warm.

Melt the chocolate in a double boiler over hot water. Whisk to smooth. Spoon melted chocolate into the corner of a plastic bag and twist to seal. Snip a tiny corner off the bag and pipe chocolate in a diagonal zigzag over each cookie.

Makes about 3 dozen.

STICKY SITUATIONS

❤ Baking parchment is the best way to get nonstick cookies. It also helps prevent spreading and makes cleanup a breeze!

LEBKUCHEN

These spiced German honey cookies are traditionally made during the holidays. They ship well, so make a double batch.

1 cup packed light-brown sugar

1/4 cup honey

1/4 cup molasses

1 large egg

finely grated zest of 1 orange

1-1/2 cups all-purpose flour

1 cup pecans or walnuts

1/2 cup raisins

1 teaspoon cinnamon

1 teaspoon nutmeg

1/2 teaspoon ground cloves

1/2 teaspoon baking soda

Combine brown sugar, honey, molasses, egg, and zest in a bowl and beat with a mixer until smooth. Set aside. Put the flour, nuts, and raisins in a food processor and process until finely chopped. Add remaining dry ingredients and process another few seconds.

Stir the dry mixture into the creamed mixture until evenly blended. Flatten dough into a 1-inch-thick square on a sheet of waxed paper. Wrap in plastic and refrigerate overnight, or up to two days.

Grease large cookie sheets and preheat oven to 350°F. Roll the dough into a 1/4-inch-thick square on a sheet of heavily floured waxed paper. Cut the dough into 2-inch squares. Place the squares onto the cookie sheets, leaving 1-1/2 inches between them. Bake for 12 to 15 minutes. When done, the cookies will form a skin but still feel soft to the touch. Cool on the sheet for 2 minutes, then transfer to a rack to cool.

Makes 18 to 22 cookies.

BEST BUTTER COOKIES

These cookies are crisp and buttery, and they keep well, if you can keep them hidden!

1 cup (2 sticks) butter, softened

1 cup sugar

1 egg

2 tablespoons orange juice

1 tablespoon vanilla extract

2-1/2 cups all-purpose flour

1 teaspoon baking powder

colored sugar (optional), for decorating

Cream butter and sugar. Add egg, orange juice, and vanilla and mix well. Add flour and baking powder. Cover dough and chill for 2 to 3 hours, or until firm. Roll out portions of the dough to 1/4 inch thick, keeping the rest chilled. Cut out with cookie cutters. Sprinkle some of the cookies with colored sugar before baking, if desired. Place onto ungreased cookie sheets and bake at 375°F for about 8 minutes, or until lightly browned. (Cool completely before frosting.)

Makes about 4 dozen.

GINGERBREAD CUTOUTS

The orange peel makes these crisp cookies extra special. The cookies freeze well, too.

1 cup (2 sticks) butter

1-1/2 cups sugar

1 egg

4 teaspoons grated orange peel (about 1 large orange)

2 teaspoons molasses or dark corn syrup

3 cups all-purpose flour

2 teaspoons baking soda

2 teaspoons cinnamon

2 teaspoons ginger

1/2 teaspoon cloves

1/2 teaspoon salt

Cream together butter and sugar. Add egg and mix well. Add grated peel and molasses and mix again. Stir together dry ingredients and add to butter mixture, stirring well. Wrap up dough and chill for several hours or overnight. Roll dough very thin and cut out with cookie cutters. Bake on greased cookie sheets at 375°F for 8 to 10 minutes.

Makes about 6 dozen, depending on size.

NOTE:

❤ **Fresh ginger and powdered ginger are very different in flavor. Do not substitute one for the other.**

SWEDISH GINGERSNAPS

These spicy cookies are the traditional Swedish Julpepparkakor *served at Christmastime. Thin, crisp, and delicious, they keep well in an airtight container.*

1/2 cup light molasses

1/2 cup (1 stick) butter, softened

1/2 cup packed dark-brown sugar

1/2 cup whipping cream

1 tablespoon cinnamon

1 tablespoon ginger

1 teaspoon ground cloves

1 teaspoon baking powder

3 to 3-1/2 cups all-purpose flour

1/2 teaspoon salt

Beat together the molasses, butter, and brown sugar until smooth. Add the cream, spices, baking powder, flour, and salt and mix well to make a stiff dough. Refrigerate for several hours or overnight. Roll out small portions of dough as thinly as possible, and cut into shapes with your favorite cookie cutters. Bake on greased cookie sheets at 375°F for about 8 minutes. Check to be sure cookies don't burn.

Makes about 5 dozen.

GERMAN HAZELNUT COOKIES

Betsy P. Race won first prize with these seasonal favorites in the 1989 Old Farmer's Almanac
Holiday Cookies and Bars Recipe Contest.

3 cups (6 sticks) ice-cold unsalted butter

3 cups all-purpose flour

3 cups unsifted confectioners' sugar

3-1/2 cups ground hazelnuts, divided

3 eggs, well beaten

juice and grated peel of 1 lemon

extra flour (up to 1 cup), for rolling

1 egg beaten with 1 tablespoon water, for glaze

Cut butter into flour as for pastry. Stir in confectioners' sugar, then 3 cups of the nuts. Add eggs, juice, and peel. Cover dough tightly with plastic wrap and chill thoroughly, for at least 2 hours. Grease baking sheets and preheat oven to 350°F. Working with a small amount of dough at a time (keep the rest of the dough refrigerated), roll out to 1/4 inch thick on a well-floured board, also dusting top of dough with flour to aid in rolling. Cut out with cookie cutters and transfer to baking sheets. (Dough may also be dropped by teaspoonfuls; cookies will flatten into brown-edged wafers as they bake.)

Brush cookies gently with egg-water mixture, and sprinkle with pinches of remaining ground nuts. Bake for 10 to 15 minutes, or until golden.

Makes about 5 to 7 dozen.

HONEY CUTOUT COOKIES

A healthy dose of whole-wheat flour gives this classic a wholesome twist. Decorate with frosting if you wish.

1 cup (2 sticks) unsalted butter, softened

1 cup packed light-brown sugar

1/2 cup honey

1 large egg

1-1/2 teaspoons vanilla extract

2 cups all-purpose flour

2 cups whole-wheat flour

1 teaspoon baking soda

1/2 teaspoon salt

2 teaspoons cinnamon

Cream the butter, brown sugar, and honey. Beat in the egg and vanilla until smooth. Sift dry ingredients and gradually stir them into the creamed mixture. Turn the dough out and knead once or twice. Divide dough in half. Flatten each half into a 1-inch-thick disk. Wrap and refrigerate for at least 2 hours or overnight.

Roll one piece of dough slightly less than 1/4 inch thick on waxed paper. Cut into shapes and place onto greased cookie sheets. Repeat for remaining dough and scraps. Bake at 350°F for 18 to 20 minutes. Cool briefly on sheets, then transfer cookies to a rack to cool.

Makes 2 to 3 dozen.

VARIATION:

■ For a wonderful flavor variation, omit the cinnamon and substitute 1/2 cup pure maple syrup for the honey.

Freezing and Storing Cookies

Because most cookies freeze well and thaw quickly, platefuls of assorted cookies can simply be covered well with plastic wrap or aluminum foil and popped into the freezer, to be brought out when company walks in the front door. (Placing un-wrapped and unfrosted cookies in a 300°F oven for a few minutes will restore crispness.) You can make your own freezer "vacuum pack": Place cookies into a plastic zipper bag, seal almost completely, and insert a straw in the corner and use it to suck out the air. Three months in the freezer is about the maximum time before cookies begin to lose flavor.

For short-term storage at room temperature, place cooled cookies into a container with a snug lid. Be sure to separate crisp and soft cookies so their respective textures will be preserved. Place layers of waxed paper between soft cookies, frosted cookies, very delicate cookies, or bars when storing or freezing them. Store soft cookies in containers with tight lids to retain moisture. Add an apple slice if necessary to add humidity. Store crisp cookies in a container with a loose-fitting lid. Well packed, your homemade cookies will keep fresh in the kitchen for about a week.

MEASURING FRUITS

Apples	1 pound (3 or 4 medium) = 3 cups sliced
Bananas	1 pound (3 or 4 medium) = 1-3/4 cups mashed
Berries	1 quart = 3-1/2 cups
Dates	1 pound = 2-1/2 cups pitted
Lemon	1 whole = 1 to 3 tablespoons juice; 1 to 1-1/2 teaspoons grated rind
Lime	1 whole = 1-1/2 to 2 tablespoons juice
Orange	1 medium = 6 to 8 tablespoons juice; 2 to 3 tablespoons grated rind
Peaches	1 pound (4 medium) = 3 cups sliced
Pears	1 pound (4 medium) = 2 cups sliced
Rhubarb	1 pound = 2 cups cooked
Strawberries	1 quart = 4 cups sliced

TEMPERATURE CONVERSION

Fahrenheit to Celsius:
Subtract 32 from the Fahrenheit number, multiply by 5, and divide by 9.

Celsius to Fahrenheit:
Multiply the Celsius number by 9, divide by 5, and add 32.

HOUSEHOLD MEASURES

pinch = about 1/8 teaspoon
120 drops of water = 1 teaspoon
60 drops thick fluid = 1 teaspoon
2 teaspoons = 1 dessertspoon
3 teaspoons = 1 tablespoon
16 tablespoons = 1 cup
8 fluid ounces = 1 cup
16 fluid ounces = 1 pint
32 fluid ounces = 1 quart
128 fluid ounces = 1 gallon
2 cups = 1 pint
2 pints = 1 quart
4 quarts = 1 gallon
2 cups granulated sugar = 1 pound
3-3/4 cups confectioners' sugar = 1 pound
2-3/4 cups brown sugar = 1 pound
3-1/2 cups wheat flour = 1 pound
5-1/3 cups dry coffee = 1 pound
4 cups cocoa = 1 pound
6-1/2 cups dry tea = 1 pound
2 cups shortening = 1 pound
3-1/2 cups walnuts (chopped) = 1 pound
9 eggs = 1 pound
3 cups cornmeal = 1 pound
2 sticks butter = 1 cup
8 egg whites = 1 cup
16 egg yolks = 1 cup
2 tablespoons sugar = 1 ounce
3 tablespoons flour = 1 ounce
2 tablespoons butter = 1 ounce
1 ounce yeast = 1 scant tablespoon

WINE MEASURES
(approximate equivalents)

1 magnum = 2/5 gallon
1 jeroboam = 4/5 gallon
1 rehoboam = 5 quarts
1 methuselah = 6-1/2 quarts
1 salmanazar = 12 quarts
1 nebuchadnezzar = 20 quarts

OLD-TIME MEASURES

60 pounds apples = 1 bushel
52 pounds beans = 1 bushel
24 pounds beets = 1 bushel
56 pounds carrots = 1 bushel
55 pounds flour = 1 bushel
54 pounds onions = 1 bushel
45 pounds parsnips = 1 bushel
50 pounds potatoes = 1 bushel
60 pounds string beans = 1 bushel
60 pounds sweet potatoes = 1 bushel
48 pounds tomatoes = 1 bushel
196 pounds turnips = 1 barrel
1 gill = 1/2 cup
1 pottle = 2 quarts
1 coomb = 4 bushels
1 wey = 40 bushels
1 last = 80 bushels
1 firkin = 9 gallons
1 anker = 10 gallons
1 runlet = 18 gallons
1 tierce = 42 gallons
1 hogshead = 63 gallons
1 puncheon = 84 gallons
1 butt = 126 gallons

METRIC MEASURES

1 teaspoon = 5 milliliters
1 tablespoon = 15 milliliters
1 cup = 240 milliliters
1 quart = 0.946 liter
1 gallon = 3.785 liters
1 liter = 1.057 quarts
1 ounce = 28.35 grams
1 pound = 454 grams
1 gram = 0.035 ounce
1 kilo = 2.205 pounds
1 inch = 2.54 centimeters
1 centimeter = 0.39 inch

Common Spices Used in Baking

ALLSPICE

Columbus found allspice (the symbol of compassion) in the West Indies in 1493. His ship's physician noted that the tree had the "finest smell of cloves" they had ever encountered. It is a member of the pepper family. In Caribbean cooking, it's known as Jamaica pepper, and in Poland, it's called *kubaba*.

- Tastes like a blend of cinnamon, nutmeg, and cloves.
- Use in pot roasts, stuffings, cakes, cookies, biscuits, pies, and relishes.

ANISE SEED

Considered good for digestion, anise was common in cough drops and in flavoring homemade spirits and tonics. In 13th-century England, the tax on anise paid for repairs to London Bridge.

- Sweet licorice flavor.
- Use in cookies, cakes, fruit fillings, and breads, or with cottage cheese, shellfish, and spaghetti dishes.

CARDAMOM, GROUND

Cardamom, related to ginger, was used in old recipes for pickled vegetables, fruits, and herring, custards, spiced wines, liqueurs, and in sauerbraten.

- Mild ginger flavor.
- It can be used in cakes and pastries (use it instead of nutmeg in pumpkin pie), curries, jellies, and sweet potatoes.

CINNAMON

An appetite stimulant, cinnamon has been used as a perfume and in sacred oils for anointing. A folklore cure for the common cold was to sniff cinnamon. Cinnamon sticks (the bark of the cinnamon tree, native to Ceylon) were used by colonial Americans as a digestive and to flavor or "mull" cider.

- Warm, spicy flavor.
- Use ground cinnamon in baked goods, stewed fruits, vegetables, spiced teas, and coffees.

CLOVES

To cure the toothache, to scent the closet, or to repel moths, colonists looked to whole cloves. They grow only near the sea, particularly in Zanzibar, Madagascar, and the West Indies. Their scent can be detected at sea even before land is sighted.

- Hot, spicy flavor.
- Use in baked goods, curries, baked beans, and beef stew, and as a pickling spice.

GINGER, GROUND

Europe had Jamaican ginger as early as 1585. It was used against plague during the Black Death. It was already used in medieval times as an ingredient of gingerbread. In the 1800s, a tincture of ginger ("digest an ounce of ginger in a pint of spirits in gentle heat for a week") was an "expellant to purgative droughts" and a cure for seasickness.

- Sweet, spicy flavor.
- Use in pies, pickles, puddings, cookies, cakes, cheese dishes, salad dressings, and soups. It's also an important ingredient in Chinese, Indian, and Arab dishes.

MACE

The dried aril of nutmeg, mace comes in pressed, flat blades when fresh. It is most commonly used ground. Old recipes used mace sparingly (often with cherries) because it was quite precious.

- Has a soft nutmeg flavor.
- Use in doughnuts and other baked goods and sauces, or with chicken, creamed fish, seafood, and fruits.

NUTMEG

Resembling the brain in appearance, nutmeg was once considered good for head ailments and eyesight. Some old-timers used nutmeg to remove freckles. In 1760, large quantities were burned in Amsterdam to keep prices high.

▪ Spicy, sweet taste.

▪ Add to sweet foods, cakes, cookies, applesauce, eggnog, soufflés, pies, custards, and meat and vegetable recipes.

POPPY SEED

A symbol of sleep, poppies grow where battles raged and where England's holy maid Margaret slew the dragon.

▪ Nutlike, sweet flavor.

▪ Good in breads, cakes, pastries, and salad dressings. Try also with vegetables and noodles.

SESAME SEED

"Open, Sesame" is what Cassim forgot in Ali Baba's tale. In East India, the seeds found culinary and ceremonial uses, including rituals for burial and fertility.

▪ Nutlike flavor when toasted.

▪ Use the white seeds in breads, rolls, and cookies. The black seeds are used in Asian cooking to coat meat and fish before cooking and to season rice and noodle dishes.

VANILLA BEAN

The pod of a climbing orchid, vanilla grows in tropical climates and was used by the Aztecs for flavoring chocolate. Frugal housewives bury chunks of it in sugar for a subtle vanilla flavor.

▪ Sweet, rich taste.

▪ Use in custards, ice cream, cookies, and pastries, and to flavor sauces.

BASIC KITCHEN EQUIPMENT

FOOD PREPARATION

Measuring cups
  Dry measure: set of 4 cups
  Wet measure: 1-cup and 2-cup
Measuring spoons
Ruler
Thermometers
  Meat
  Candy/frying
  Freezer
Timer
Mixing bowls (3 sizes)
Chopping board
Knives
  Chef's knife
  Paring knife
  Bread knife (serrated edge)
  Carving knife
Knife sharpener
Kitchen shears
Vegetable parer
Openers
  Bottle opener
  Corkscrew
  Jar opener
  Can opener
Pepper grinder
Rotary eggbeater
Nutcracker
Funnel
Grater
Colander
Strainer
Juicer

COOKING

Pots, skillets, and pans
  Saucepans:
  1- to 2-cup,
  1-quart, 2-quart,
  and 8-quart
Skillets/frying pans:
  7-inch, 10-inch, and 12-inch
Griddle
Flameproof casserole or Dutch oven
Casseroles and baking dishes
Roasting pan (with rack)
Double boiler
Steamer
Kettle
Coffeepot
Wooden spoons
Rubber spatula
Metal utensils
  Metal spatula
  Slotted spoon
  Cooking fork
  Ladle
  Potato masher
  Tongs
  Whisk
Skewers
Bulb baster
Brush

BAKING

Pastry blender
Rolling pin
Sifter
Cake pans
  Pair of 8- or 9-inch round
  8- or 9-inch square
  13x9-inch rectangular
  10-inch tube
Loaf pans
Cookie sheets (at least 2)
Jelly-roll pan
Muffin tins
Pie pans
Custard cups
Cooling racks

Substitutions for Common Ingredients

ITEM	QUANTITY	SUBSTITUTION
Allspice	1 teaspoon	1/2 teaspoon cinnamon plus 1/8 teaspoon ground cloves
Arrowroot, as thickener	1-1/2 teaspoons	1 tablespoon flour
Baking powder	1 teaspoon	1/4 teaspoon baking soda plus 5/8 teaspoon cream of tartar
Bread crumbs, dry	1/4 cup	1 slice bread
Bread crumbs, soft	1/2 cup	1 slice bread
Buttermilk	1 cup	1 cup plain yogurt
Chocolate, unsweetened	1 ounce	3 tablespoons cocoa plus 1 tablespoon butter or fat
Cracker crumbs	3/4 cup	1 cup dry bread crumbs
Cream, heavy	1 cup	3/4 cup milk plus 1/3 cup melted butter (this will not whip)
Cream, light	1 cup	7/8 cup milk plus 3 tablespoons melted butter
Cream, sour	1 cup	7/8 cup buttermilk or plain yogurt plus 3 tablespoons melted butter
Cream, whipping	1 cup	2/3 cup well-chilled evaporated milk, whipped; **or** 1 cup nonfat dry milk powder whipped with 1 cup ice water
Flour, all-purpose	1 cup	1-1/8 cups cake flour; **or** 5/8 cup potato flour; **or** 1-1/4 cups rye flour or coarsely ground whole-grain flour; **or** 1 cup cornmeal
Flour, cake	1 cup	1 cup minus 2 tablespoons sifted all-purpose flour
Flour, self-rising	1 cup	1 cup all-purpose flour plus 1-1/4 teaspoons baking powder plus 1/4 teaspoon salt
Garlic	1 small clove	1/8 teaspoon garlic powder or instant minced garlic
Herbs, dried	1/2 to 1 teaspoon	1 tablespoon fresh herbs, minced and packed
Honey	1 cup	1-1/4 cups sugar plus 1/2 cup liquid
Lemon juice	1 teaspoon	1/2 teaspoon vinegar
Lemon, juice and rind	1	3 tablespoons bottled lemon juice and 1 teaspoon dried grated rind

ITEM	QUANTITY	SUBSTITUTION
Lemon rind, grated	1 teaspoon	1/2 teaspoon lemon extract
Milk, skim	1 cup	1/3 cup instant nonfat dry milk plus 3/4 cup water
Milk, to sour	1 cup	1 cup minus 1 tablespoon milk plus 1 tablespoon vinegar or lemon juice. Stir and let stand 5 minutes.
Milk, whole	1 cup	1/2 cup evaporated milk plus 1/2 cup water; **or** 1 cup skim milk plus 2 teaspoons melted butter
Mustard, prepared	1 tablespoon	1 teaspoon dry or powdered mustard
Onion, chopped	1 small	1 tablespoon instant minced onion; **or** 1 teaspoon onion powder; **or** 1/4 cup frozen chopped onion
Sugar, granulated	1 cup	1 cup firmly packed brown sugar; **or** 1-3/4 cups confectioners' sugar (do not substitute in baking); **or** 1/2 cup honey; **or** 1 cup superfine sugar; **or** 1-1/2 cups corn syrup; **or** 2/3 cup maple syrup (for last two, reduce liquid in recipe by 25 percent)
Tomatoes, canned	1 cup	1/2 cup tomato sauce plus 1/2 cup water; **or** 1-1/3 cups chopped fresh tomatoes, simmered
Tomato juice	1 cup	1/2 cup tomato sauce plus 1/2 cup water plus dash each salt and sugar; **or** 1/4 cup tomato paste plus 3/4 cup water plus salt and sugar, to taste
Tomato ketchup	1/2 cup	1/2 cup tomato sauce plus 2 tablespoons sugar, 1 tablespoon vinegar, and 1/8 teaspoon ground cloves
Tomato puree	1 cup	1/2 cup tomato paste plus 1/2 cup water
Tomato soup	1 can (10-3/4 oz.)	1 cup tomato sauce plus 1/4 cup water
Vanilla	1-inch bean	1 teaspoon vanilla extract
Yeast	1 cake (3/5 oz.)	1 package active dry yeast
Yogurt, plain	1 cup	1 cup buttermilk

My Favorite Cookie Recipes

COOKIE NAME

INGREDIENTS

DIRECTIONS

COOKIE NAME

INGREDIENTS

DIRECTIONS

Cookie Name

Ingredients

Directions

Cookie Name

Ingredients

Directions

COOKIE NAME

INGREDIENTS

DIRECTIONS

COOKIE NAME

INGREDIENTS

DIRECTIONS

COOKIE NAME

INGREDIENTS

DIRECTIONS

COOKIE NAME

INGREDIENTS

DIRECTIONS

COOKIE NAME

INGREDIENTS

DIRECTIONS

COOKIE NAME

INGREDIENTS

DIRECTIONS

COOKIE NAME

INGREDIENTS

DIRECTIONS

COOKIE NAME

INGREDIENTS

DIRECTIONS

Cookie Name

Ingredients

Directions

Cookie Name

Ingredients

Directions

COOKIE NAME

INGREDIENTS

DIRECTIONS

COOKIE NAME

INGREDIENTS

DIRECTIONS

Cookie Notes

 *Use this section to keep track of your family's and friends' favorite cookies, to help you remember which ones you took to the office party last year and which cookies Uncle Henry really hates!*

Acknowledgments

Ken Haedrich

Ken first got the idea that a man's place might be in the kitchen by watching his father make apple pies. The father of four children himself, Ken finds that making cookies just comes naturally. And he says that his kids are his best critics. Ken has written numerous cookbooks, including Country Baking: Simple Home Baking with Wholesome Grains and the Pick of the Harvest *and* Home for the Holidays: Festive Baking with Whole Grains *(both from Galahad Books).*

Flo Braker

Flo specializes in American and European baking and pastrymaking as well as chocolate work, and her trademark is her extraordinary variety of sweet miniatures. Besides being featured in such magazines as Bon Appetit, Chocolatier, *and* Woman's Day, *Flo has been teaching baking techniques across the country for 25 years. Flo's books include* The Simple Art of Perfect Baking *(Houghton-Mifflin) and the newly updated and revised* Sweet Miniatures: The Art of Making Bite-Size Desserts *(Chronicle Books).*

Susan Peery

Susan has been making cookies with great enthusiasm from an early age, a happy circumstance for which she thanks her mother, Margaret Mahnke, who taught her how. (Susan has continued the tradition by teaching her children, Molly and Spencer, the joys of cookie-making.) Former managing editor of The Old Farmer's Almanac *and former food editor of* Yankee *Magazine, Susan is also the author of several cookbooks:* The Wellesley Cookie Exchange Cookbook *(Simon & Schuster, Inc.) and* Potluck Plain & Fancy *(Alan Hood), written with her husband, Gordon Peery.*